Table of Contents

Improving Reading Comprehension
Grade 6
Introduction

Introduction

We have all watched a child struggle while learning to read. Each new word can be a challenge or a frustration. We have joined in the child's struggle, teaching the skills needed to decode unfamiliar words and make sense of the letters. Then we have experienced joy as the child mastered the words and began to read sentences, gaining confidence with each new success.

Learning to read is one of the most important skills students ever acquire. By the sixth grade, most children are independent, confident readers. The emphasis now can be placed on practicing the valuable skills of reading comprehension. When a child reads without understanding, he or she will quickly become disinterested. Readers need to develop the skill of making sense of new words through context. They need to understand an author's message, whether stated or implied. They need to see how each event in a story affects the rest of the story and its characters. These are all important skills that must be nurtured if a student is to be a successful reader. Reading comprehension is vital throughout the school curriculum and for success in many other areas of life.

To build the necessary skills for reading comprehension, a reading program should clear away other stresses so that the student can concentrate on the reading. Keeping that in mind, the stories in *Improving Reading Comprehension* have been written to interest and engage the readers. They are short to hold the reader's attention.

The exercises are short but effective tools to determine the student's understanding of each story. Given as homework or class work, the two-page assignments can easily be incorporated into existing reading programs for practice and reinforcement of reading comprehension skills.

Organization

The stories in *Improving Reading Comprehension* have been divided into six chapters: School Days, A Tale to Tell, It Takes All Kinds, You Never Know..., Using Your Head, and Figuring It Out. The stories are a mix of fantasy, nonfiction, and realistic fiction.

Each story includes one or two comprehension exercises. These exercises concentrate on the student's understanding of the story. Many exercises emphasize vocabulary as well. The exercises include completing sentences, matching words with definitions, writing, finding words with similar meanings, multiple-choice questions, cloze, and crossword puzzles. Each story and its exercise(s) are complete on two sides of one tear-out sheet.

The Curriculum Correlation Chart on page 4 will allow you to include the reading in other curriculum areas.

There is a Letter to Parents on page 5, and a Letter to Students is on page 6. Notifying students and parents of a new activity beforehand will help answer students' questions and keep parents informed.

There are two assessments. Each assessment can be used individually or paired with the other and given in any order.

Use

Improving Reading Comprehension is designed for independent use by students. Copies of the stories and activities can be given to individual students, pairs of students, or small groups for completion. They can also be used as a center activity.

To begin, determine the implementation that fits your students' needs and your classroom structure. The following plan suggests a format for this implementation.

1. **Explain** the purpose of the activities to your class.

2. **Review** the mechanics of how you want students to work with the exercises. You may wish to introduce the subject of each article. You may decide to tap into students' prior knowledge of the subject for discussion. You might plan a group discussion after the reading.

3. **Remind** students that they are reading for understanding. Tell them to read carefully. Remind them to use a dictionary when necessary if the context is not enough to help them figure out a word.

4. **Determine** how you will monitor the assessments. Each assessment is designed to be used independently. You may decide to administer the assessments to the whole class, to

small groups who have completed a unit, or to individuals as they work through the book. The assessments can be used as pre- and post-evaluations of the students' progress.

Additional Notes

1. **Parent Communication.** Use the Letter to Parents, and encourage the students to share the Letter to Students with their parents. Decide if you want to keep the activity pages and assessments in portfolios for conferencing or if you want students to take them home as they are completed.

2. **Bulletin Boards.** Since a key to comprehension is discussion, encourage students to illustrate, add to, or do further research on their favorite stories. Display the students' work on a bulletin board.

3. **Have Fun.** Reading should be fun, and the stories in *Improving Reading Comprehension* will capture students' interest and stimulate their imagination. Fun group discussions, ideas, or games that evolve from the reading will enhance the learning experience.

Improving Reading Comprehension
Grade 6

Curriculum Correlation

Story Title	Social Studies	Language Arts	Science	Math	Physical Education
Language Limbo	X	X			
A Hero at Home	X	X			
Poetry Puzzles		X			
Practical Prize		X	X		
The Trouble with William	X	X			
An Old New Idea	X	X			
Saved by the Bell	X	X			
Fox's Tale	X	X			
Casey Jones		X			
Ghostly Tales		X			
A Bit of Finn	X	X			
Tran's Secret	X	X			
Telling Tales	X	X			
Those Little Lies	X	X			X
Stealing Home	X	X			X
It's How You Look at It	X	X	X		
A Stray to Stay		X			
A Good Guide		X			
Looking for Trouble	X	X			
A World of Difference	X	X			
Babysitting Blues		X			
Hector the Hero	X	X	X		
Never Say Never	X	X			
Time Travel		X		X	
One More Night		X			X
Alyson's Wish		X			
Little Louisa		X		X	
Another Person's Shoes	X	X			
Rhino's Return		X			X
Tracking Tess		X			
Recipe Rewards		X			
Vegetable Void		X		X	
Taping Time		X		X	
Party Surprise		X			X
Just Plane Crazy		X		X	
An Eye for Detail		X		X	
Burglar Bungle		X			
Celia's Scare		X			
Lost Louis		X			
Alfonso's New Home		X			
Troy's Home!		X			
Dragging Her Feet		X			

Dear Parents:

Learning to read is clearly one of the most important things your child will ever do. By the sixth grade, most children are confident, independent readers. They have developed a large vocabulary and have learned ways to understand the meanings of some unfamiliar words through context.

What is equally important for all readers, however, is reading with understanding. If your child reads a story but is unable to describe the events in his or her own words or answer questions about the story, then the reading loses its meaning. Young readers need practice to strengthen their reading comprehension abilities.

With this goal in mind, our class will be working with a book of stories and activities that will reinforce reading comprehension. The short stories are a mix of fiction and nonfiction. The stories are fun, and the one-page exercises are varied. Without feeling the pressure of a long story to remember or many pages of exercises to work, your child will develop a better understanding of the reading and have fun doing it!

Occasionally, your child may bring home an activity. Please consider the following suggestions to help your child work successfully.

- Provide a quiet place to work.
- If your child is reading, help to find the meanings of difficult words through the context of the story. Discuss the story.
- Go over the directions for the exercises together.
- Check the lesson when it is complete. Note areas of improvement as well as concern.

Thank you for being involved with your child's learning. A strong reading foundation will lead to a lifetime of reading enjoyment and success.

Cordially,

Dear Student:

Have you read a good book lately? You can probably describe in detail many of the scenes in the book. Maybe your mind returns often to some of the characters. If you enjoyed the book, you probably told a friend or someone in your family about it. It is helpful to think and talk about what you have read. This can help you to remember, to understand your reading, and perhaps to think about it in new ways.

We will be working with a book of short stories. After reading each one, you will be asked to think about the story. Then you will answer some questions. Thinking about these stories will help you become a better, more confident reader.

The stories are a mix of facts and fun. There are stories of school and stories about people in new, challenging, or intriguing situations. Read carefully and have fun. There is a story here for everyone!

Sincerely,

Assessment 1

Directions

Read the paragraphs. Then follow the directions for each exercise.

Wandering along the creek behind our house, I was preoccupied with the subject of the next paper I had to write for English class. Heroes had always seemed to me like people who lived in another world; certainly, they were people whom I would never get the chance to meet.

Take heroes like Paul Bunyan and Davy Crockett, for instance. Even though one was a folk hero and one was a real person, they both performed deeds that no ordinary human being could hope to accomplish. And then there are the heroes who go down in history, like great presidents, prime ministers, and astronauts. Are they heroes because they are part of history, or because they just did what they had to do in their very public jobs?

And what about the occasional heroes, those who surface unexpectedly when injured people need to be pulled from wrecked airplanes or when little children fall down abandoned wells? These heroes all seem to be recognized for specific admirable deeds. Are they heroes all their lives or just for their momentary courage during a time of crisis?

Choose the word that best fits each sentence. Write the word in the blank.

1. Walking along the creek, I was _____ with thoughts of my next paper.
   precious   happy   preoccupied

2. Public people, like presidents and prime _____, go down in history books.
   minstrels   ministers   astronauts

3. Some heroes seem to be recognized for specific _____ deeds.
   admirable   admiring   admitting

4. Are they heroes only for their _____ courage?
   momentary   moment   memory

5. Some people become heroes during times of _____ .
   joy   caring   crisis

Go on to next page.

Directions

Answer each question about the story. Circle the letter in front of the correct answer.

6. Why did the writer feel that heroes were from another world?
   a. because they were usually aliens
   b. because he would never meet them
   c. because they go down in history
   d. because they surface unexpectedly

7. What do Paul Bunyan and Davy Crockett have in common?
   a. They were both real people.
   b. They were both folk heroes.
   c. They both performed incredible deeds.
   d. They were both presidents.

8. The writer wonders whether presidents are heroes because _____.
   a. they are all incredibly brave
   b. they do what they have to do
   c. everyone thinks they can do no wrong
   d. only heroes can be presidents

Rewrite each sentence. Use a word with the same meaning from the passage in place of the underlined words.

9. Heroes can surface <u>when they are not expected</u> in times of crisis.

   _____

10. My mind had been <u>spending all its time</u> with thoughts of heroes.

   _____

11. Many heroes are recognized for specific <u>inspiring admiration</u> deeds.

   _____

Write about someone who is a hero to you. It can be someone known to you or someone about whom you have heard. Use four to five complete sentences. Use another piece of paper, if necessary.

   _____

   _____

   _____

Assessment 2

Directions

Read the paragraphs. Then follow the directions for each exercise.

There is a story told of a town in England. Loud, piercing noises assaulted the people for years. Then they stopped as suddenly and mysteriously as they had begun. Sometimes the noise took the form of a high-pitched hum, heard by many. At other times, a crushing pressure accompanied it. This affected individual people and groups and caused them great pain and suffering before it stopped. The high-pitched whistle even stunned a flock of birds in mid-flight. They all fell to the ground, dead. Cats and dogs were affected by the noise as well, probably due to their fine hearing.

Many scientists and experts on ghostly activity have studied the area. They have tried to ascertain the cause for these disturbances. No one has ever come up with an explanation. As with most ghostly activity, it remains a mystery.

Read each sentence. Choose a word from the story that has the same meaning as the word or words in bold print. Write the word on the line.

1. Loud noises **attacked** the people of the town for years. _____

2. A piercing whistle stunned a flock of birds in **the middle of their flight**. _____

3. Experts have tried to **determine** the cause of these sounds. _____

4. No one has come up with an **answer to explain something**. _____

5. The **commotions, or disorders,** remain a mystery. _____

Go on to next page.

Directions

Think about the story you read. Then fill in the blanks of the following paragraph with words from the story.

In a town in England, people were **6)** _____ with loud noises for years before

they stopped as mysteriously as they had begun. The noise could be a **7)** _____

hum. At times, it was **8)** _____ by a great pressure. The whistling stunned

and killed a group of birds in **9)** _____. Although experts have tried to

10) _____ the cause of these disturbances, the noises remain a mystery.

Write _true_ or _false_ next to each sentence about the story.

11. _____ The story takes place in Scotland.

12. _____ The noises affected groups of people as well as individuals.

13. _____ Animals were affected by the noises.

14. _____ Scientists have since discovered the cause for the disturbances.

15. _____ Most ghostly activity can be explained.

Write about something that has been a mystery to you. It can be something that is no longer a mystery or something that is still unexplained. Tell why it is or is not a mystery now. Use four to five complete sentences.

_____

_____

_____

_____

Language Limbo

When she first learned that they could come to the United States, Eddie's mother had begun trying to teach him English. She was still trying on the day they took the big jet airplane to America.

Eddie had learned things quickly in school in Vietnam, but he just didn't understand how important it would soon be for him to know English. When he got to Iowa, he discovered that his father and all the other people he saw in Iowa spoke English.

It was awful at first. The children at school seemed to want to be his friends, but he couldn't talk to them or understand what was going on in class. He couldn't read any of the books everyone used. Most importantly, he couldn't tell anyone how he felt.

His mother spoke to him in English. She wanted him to communicate with others besides her, so she used Vietnamese only to explain what English words meant. Eddie had never felt so alone. His father would put an arm around Eddie, speaking very slowly; but that didn't help Eddie understand what his father said.

One day in math class, Eddie suddenly realized that he understood what the teacher was saying. From that day on, things got easier for him; but he was confused when his mother began speaking in Vietnamese again. "You're lucky to have two languages," she explained, "so you must always practice them both."

Go on to next page.

Directions

Answer each question about the story. Circle the letter in front of the correct answer.

1. Eddie needs to learn English because _____.
   a. he lives in Vietnam
   b. he is moving to Iowa
   c. his father sends him books in English
   d. his mother is from Iowa

2. Eddie can't communicate with other people in Iowa because they _____.
   a. are all speaking English
   b. don't want to be friendly
   c. all speak two languages
   d. leave him alone at home

3. Eddie's mother will not speak to him in Vietnamese because she is _____.
   a. embarrassed to use it in the United States
   b. trying to forget the language
   c. unable to speak it
   d. trying to get Eddie to use English

4. Eddie finally begins to understand English one day when _____.
   a. his father is talking to him
   b. he is in mathematics class
   c. a teacher speaks Vietnamese
   d. his mother explains to him about English

5. Eddie's mother begins to speak to him in Vietnamese again because she _____.
   a. saw that he will never learn English
   b. is feeling lonely, too
   c. does not want him to forget it
   d. forgets how to speak English

A Hero at Home

Wandering along the creek behind our house, I was preoccupied with thoughts about heroes, the subject of the next paper I had to write for English class. Heroes had always seemed to me like people who lived in another world; certainly, they were people whom I would never get the chance to meet.

Take heroes like Paul Bunyan and Davy Crockett, for instance. Even though one was a folk hero and one was a real person, they both performed deeds that no ordinary human could hope to accomplish. And then there are the heroes who go down in history, like great presidents, prime ministers, and astronauts. Are they heroes because they are part of history, or because they just did what they had to do in their very public jobs?

And what about the occasional heroes, those who surface unexpectedly when injured people need to be pulled from wrecked airplanes or when little children fall down abandoned wells? These heroes all seem to be recognized for specific admirable deeds. Are they heroes all of their lives or just for their momentary courage during a time of crisis?

I was feeling some anxiety about the subject until, suddenly, I stopped in my tracks. I had just thought of the most wonderful hero! He is someone I know, someone whose daily acts of courage are often performed when he is bone-weary from an exhausting day. He is my dad. Dad is so good at everything that everyone wants his help. He is so constantly in demand at home, at the office, and in our community that he hardly ever has time for himself. Yet he makes time for us children no matter what else is scheduled. He is the most  attentive listener I have ever known, and somehow every time I go to him for guidance or help with a problem, I always end up feeling like a hero myself. It is as though his air of confidence spills over from him onto anyone who approaches him.

I don't think I'll have any difficulty in writing about heroes now. I think I'll just write about my dad.

Go on to next page.

Name _____   Date _____

Directions

Think about the passage you read. Then fill in the blanks of the following paragraph with words from the Word List.

Word List

preoccupied   momentary   crisis   attentive
admirable   guidance   anxiety   prime ministers

As I walked along, my mind was **1)** _____ with thoughts of heroes.

When I thought of heroes, I thought of well-known people—rulers such as presidents and

2) _____. I thought of those who were recognized for their

3) _____ acts of courage during times of **4)** _____.

Were they heroes only during their **5)** _____ acts of courage, or all of their

lives? Then I thought of someone whose **6)** _____ listening and whose

7) _____ I have depended upon for so many things. My

8) _____ about the writing project vanished when I realized I already knew

a hero—my dad!

Use the Word List above to choose the correct word for each meaning. Write your choice on the line.

9. with all one's attention _____

10. for a short time _____

11. absorbed in thought _____

12. a time of great danger _____

13. advice _____

14. to be praised _____

15. concern _____

16. governmental chief _____

Poetry Puzzles

The members of Miss Summer's class were writing poems. Each poem was a figure of speech that described something. As they finished writing, the students took turns reading their work aloud. Each student who identified a figure of speech was allowed to read his or her own poem. Perry began with this poem.

I open it like a present to give
to my little brother, who crawls up
and sits near
my gift of animals that live
as I read the stories he wants to hear.

Anna guessed Perry's poem, so she read hers.

It roars at me to get out of the way
when I loaf in the house on Saturday.
It eats up the dirt and all of the dust
and growls, "Get busy! You must! You must!"
It pulls my father around on its cord
and makes such a racket you can't hear a word.

Hal finally got that one and then read his own poem.

When I watch the parade, I wait to see
the huge golden mirrors reflecting me
from the back of the band, and flashing high
as the sun burns brightly in each big eye.
"Crash!" and "Crash! We see you blinking!"
"Keep clapping and playing!" is what I'm thinking.

Go on to next page.

Directions

Answer each question about the story. Circle the letter in front of each correct answer.

1. Anna guesses that Perry is describing _____.
   a. a toy he gives to his brother
   b. the ribbon on a package
   c. a cage at the zoo
   d. a book he reads to his brother

2. The object Perry describes is compared to a _____.
   a. little boy
   b. pet dog
   c. gift to be opened
   d. door that is closed

3. Hal guesses that Anna's poem is about _____.
   a. her pet dog
   b. a vacuum cleaner
   c. a kite
   d. her baby brother

4. Hal's poem describes _____.
   a. cymbals
   b. airplanes
   c. windows
   d. glasses

5. The objects in Hal's poem are compared to _____.
   a. mirrors and eyes
   b. flags carried in a parade
   c. helicopters
   d. cameras

Practical Prize

Anne's preferred subjects to study had always been ones that had to do with people. She liked history and sociology, but studying about bugs, germs, or chemicals had never won her interest.

This year, the fifth and sixth grades had to develop a scientific project to present at a science fair. Anne was a high achiever, but all she ever did was complain about science. She wondered if she had the background to complete even the simplest project. Her friends were all solving impossible problems. They were showing how to make plastic, growing tomatoes in sand, building systems for electricity, and planning mazes for mice to run through.

Anne decided that her friends were much braver than she was, but she didn't want to give up. She decided to visit the science museum to see if she could get an idea. Anne was interested in improving the quality of life for people. She was impressed by an exhibit with the title, "Help Your Children Breathe More Easily." It was about the conservation of natural resources.

Anne reviewed the exhibit carefully until she had an exact idea of what she would do. She made an "Energy Detective Game" for children to play at home. Through its activities, children learned how they could save money by turning off radios and stereos. They used clues and guessed where the greatest losses occurred. Anne's project was a great success, and she won a prize for the most practical project!

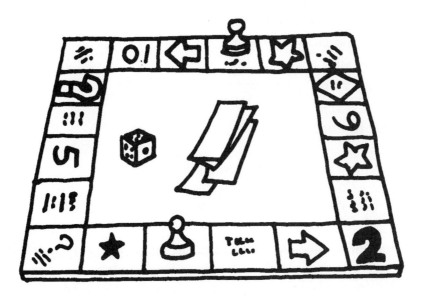

Go on to next page.

Name _____   Date _____

Directions ————————————————————————

Answer each question about the story. Circle the letter in front of the correct answer.

1. Anne preferred to study about _____.
    a. insects and germs
    b. people
    c. chemicals
    d. science

2. How did Anne describe her friends for taking on such impossible projects?
    a. brave
    b. strong
    c. foolish
    d. intelligent

3. What did Anne do to get an idea?
    a. She asked her friends for ideas.
    b. She asked her parents to help her.
    c. She went to the science museum.
    d. She went for a walk in the woods.

4. Why was Anne's project described as *practical*?
    a. It was the only project about conservation.
    b. It was a project for children to use.
    c. It was the only project that made sense.
    d. It was a project that served a useful purpose.

Write *true* or *false* next to each sentence.

5. _____ Anne was a high achiever in school.

6. _____ Anne felt comfortable with science.

7. _____ At first, Anne did not feel that she could do a science project.

8. _____ Some students were going to grow potatoes in sand.

9. _____ The museum had an exhibit on conservation of natural resources.

10. _____ Anne made an exhibit for the fair just like the one at the museum.

The Trouble with William

"I can't believe it!" cried Mrs. Johnson as she hung up the phone. She turned to her husband, who had looked up from his newspaper at her exclamation. "That was my sister, June," she explained. "She says that the teachers from William's new school are complaining about his work there."

"Complaining about *William*?" Mr. Johnson replied incredulously. "I don't believe it! He's such a good student!"

"I know!" exclaimed Mrs. Johnson. "But June said that the principal of the school called her and discussed his daydreaming and drawing. They agreed that William was very creative, even inventive, but they said he wasn't concentrating on what he needed to do there."

As Mr. and Mrs. Johnson continued talking about William, Allan, who had overheard their discussion, became upset and wandered off to his room. He didn't want to hear any more.

William had been Allan's favorite cousin ever since the two were very young. They were about the same age; and since they lived near each other, they spent a great deal of time together. William and Allan were very different, but they hardly ever argued because they complemented one another. Allan was the bold, active one, always looking for adventure. William was the quiet, playfully inventive one, who always thought up things to make or do that would not have occurred to Allan in a million years. Allan admired William so strongly that he always pictured his cousin becoming another Einstein or Picasso or Mozart. It hardly seemed possible that teachers would object to a student like William.

Go on to next page.

Directions

Answer each question about the story. Circle the letter in front of the correct answer.

1. Mrs. Johnson was talking to _____ on the telephone.
   a. William's teachers
   b. her sister, June
   c. Mr. Johnson
   d. Allan's teachers

2. Mr. Johnson described William as a _____.
   a. good student
   b. creative student
   c. daydreamer
   d. poor student

3. Mr. Johnson replied *incredulously* because he _____.
   a. thought it was funny
   b. agreed with the teachers
   c. was upset about William
   d. couldn't believe what he heard

4. Allan was upset because _____.
   a. he held William in such high regard
   b. he knew the teachers would call about him next
   c. he felt he would never see William again
   d. he found out that William was not bold or inventive

5. William needs to _____.
   a. stop being creative
   b. pay attention in school
   c. visit his cousin more
   d. give up his drawing

An Old New Idea

Many parents today are joining a movement to teach their children at home. This "new" idea, called home schooling, seems new to us because we are used to thinking of students in a traditional school setting. Many years ago, however, the majority of children who received an education learned at home. Nevertheless, the reasons that parents are trying home schooling today are not the same as they were then.

Many schools are becoming more crowded. As class sizes grow, teachers have less time to spend with individual students. Many parents believe that they can give their children more specialized and individual attention at home. Many parents are also concerned about what is being taught at school. They may feel that the basics are being buried under all of the other subjects that have been added to today's curriculum. Some parents also worry about today's school environments. In many schools, teachers spend much of their time controlling violence and disciplining students. Some students are afraid of others. This environment is not one to encourage learning.

Not everyone agrees that home schooling is a good idea, however. Most parents do not have the training that teachers do. They may not be aware of the different methods that can be employed in teaching. If a child is not getting the information one way, there are other ways to teach the same concepts. At home, children will not be able to measure their progress against that of their peers. There is also the concern that a child at home may feel isolated. The child may not develop the social skills he or she will need with other children.

Home schooling is not for every student, nor is it for every parent. But more parents increasingly feel that public schools are not the best choice. It is likely that the issue will be debated for some time.

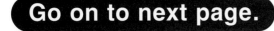
Go on to next page.

Name_____   Date_____

Directions

Read each clue. Choose a word from the story that best fits each clue. Write the words in the puzzle.

ACROSS

3. core of subjects taught at school
5. apart from others
6. most of a group
7. used

DOWN

1. more and more
2. for a particular reason or person
3. ideas; lessons
4. physical acts to cause injury or damage

Saved by the Bell

Jeremy paced back and forth in his room, then walked downstairs to the kitchen and stood with the refrigerator door open for several minutes. He closed the door and looked around. Today was the first day of school, but Jeremy wasn't going to be there. His family was going to England for two months because of his father's job. His parents felt it would be an enriching experience for Jeremy, so they didn't mind his starting school late. He would be mailed some assignments to work on while he was in England.

Jeremy anticipated the trip with excitement, and he knew how fortunate he was to have this chance to travel, but he felt very strange not going to school with his friends. This was the time of year when you left for school with new notebooks and pens. You got to see all the friends that had been gone all summer and catch up on the news. He could hardly believe it, but he actually resented the fact that he wasn't sitting at a desk right now, taking notes on some new subject. He imagined the joking and camaraderie of the cafeteria and pictured his friends laughing in the halls and working together in the library. He hoped his friends would leave a space for him until he got back. Would they still want to hang out with him, or would they find some other kid to take his place? He shook his head; he knew he was just being paranoid, but it was hard to be sitting here at home just waiting!

After school, he met up with his friends to talk about what they had done, who their teachers were, and all the news he had missed. He listened to everything with thinly concealed envy. Of course, his friends wished they were going to England like Jeremy—he didn't even try to explain his feelings to them.

That evening during dinner, the telephone rang. His mother answered it and didn't return to the table until Jeremy was finishing his dessert. "Well, that was your dad," she said with a resigned look. "It seems you'll be going to school tomorrow after all. His company is postponing his trip until spring. I'm sorry, honey."

"Hey, it's all right, Mom," said Jeremy, with an immense feeling of relief. "Don't worry about me!"

Go on to next page.

Name _____   Date _____

Directions

Answer each question about the story. Circle the letter in front of the correct answer.

1. Jeremy is feeling strange because he _____.
   a. is going to England
   b. is not in school with his friends
   c. can't find anything to eat
   d. is alone in his house

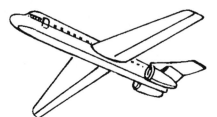

2. Jeremy is surprised because _____.
   a. he is looking forward to his trip
   b. his friends do not miss him
   c. the school has not called
   d. he actually misses taking notes

3. Why does Jeremy think he is being paranoid?
   a. He is worried that his plane will crash.
   b. He is afraid that his assignments will not reach him.
   c. He is concerned that his friends will forget about him.
   d. He thinks he will not know what to do in England.

4. Why doesn't Jeremy tell his friends how he is feeling?
   a. He doesn't think they will understand.
   b. He doesn't think they will be interested.
   c. He doesn't know how to express his feelings.
   d. He doesn't know them very well.

5. Is it likely that in the spring, Jeremy will be more willing to leave for England because _____?
   a. he will be able to bring his friends
   b. he will be ready for something new
   c. he will have met some people from England
   d. he will be tired of his friends

Fox's Tale

A fox had the misfortune to have his bushy tail caught in a trap. When he saw that it was a question of his life or his tail, he left his tail behind him. He felt himself disgraced, however, and for a time did not go near his friends for fear of ridicule.

But one day the idea came to him how he could make the best of a bad bargain. He called a meeting of all the rest of the foxes and proposed to them that they should follow his example.

"You have no idea," he said, "of the ease and comfort I am enjoying. I don't know why I didn't cut off my tail long ago. I could never have believed it if I had not tried it myself. When you come to think about it, friends, a tail is such an inconvenient and unnecessary appendage that it is strange we have put up with it so long. My sincere advice to you all is to share this new freedom and part with your tails at once."

As he concluded, one of the older and wiser foxes stepped forward and said: "There is not one of us who does not believe that you found it convenient to cut off your tail. However, we are not so convinced that you would advise us to part with our tails if there were any chance of recovering your own."

Directions

Answer each question about the fable. Circle the letter in front of the correct answer.

1. The fox cuts off his tail because he _____.
   a. thinks he looks fashionable without it
   b. doesn't want to have to groom it
   c. has to get out of a trap
   d. thinks it is inconvenient

2. The fox doesn't see many of the other foxes for some time because he is _____.
   a. caught in a trap
   b. letting his injured tail mend and heal
   c. trying to find the trap that took his tail
   d. embarrassed to be seen without his tail

3. The fox wants the other foxes to _____.
   a. cut off their tails
   b. value their tails highly
   c. steer clear of traps
   d. help him find a new tail

4. After the fox presents his argument, the other foxes are _____.
   a. polite but suspicious
   b. thankful for the advice
   c. angry that he tried to trick them
   d. happy without tails

5. The moral of the story is _____.
   a. *never cut off your nose to spite your face*
   b. *misery loves company*
   c. *stay in your burrow at all times*
   d. *keep your eye on the chicken coop*

Casey Jones

Engine No. 382 began to roll. It was heading south along the steel rails out of the South Memphis yards. From the cab window, John Luther Jones sighted down the right-of-way. His hand was on the throttle that governed the speed of the black smoke-coughing locomotive. Those were the glory days of railroading. The lines worked hard to get freight, and train speed was important. The men like Casey Jones who drove the trains up, down, and across the country were thought of as heroes living in a separate world.

The strength and daring of the six-foot four-inch Casey had already inspired one railroad song. It told of his deed of racing past a crack Limited Mail train while driving an engine supposed to be much slower. Another happening added to his good name. When he was coming into the Memphis yards one morning, a little girl ran into the path of his train and froze with fright. Casey spotted her, shouted to his fireman to take over, and ran forward on the engine's catwalk. He dropped to the cowcatcher and caught up the little girl just before the train reached her.

As he left Memphis on the fateful morning of April 30, 1893, he was on his way to even greater fame. Between Durant and Canton stood a small station named Vaughn. Here two long freight trains had turned off onto a siding in order to clear the right-of-way. Their two lengths, however, were too much for the siding, and a caboose and two cars hung over the main track. As No. 382 sliced through a thick fog, Casey spotted the caboose's rear lights. He knew that at his speed a crash was sure to come. He yelled to his fireman to jump from the cab. In one motion, he pushed the throttle in, forced the air brake all the way down, and slammed open the sandbox to snuff out the fire in the boiler. There was no escape for him,
however, and he knew it. With its whistle blowing, No. 382 plowed into the caboose, sending wood and metal flying. It broke into the next car, from which poured bales of hay. Then the locomotive tore loose and leaped from the track. Dead under his engine lay Casey Jones. He was the only one to die. Still not broken was his record of never having been in an accident in which a fellow worker or passenger was lost.

Go on to next page.

Name_____ Date_____

Directions

Rewrite each sentence. Use a word with the same meaning from the Word List in place of the underlined words.

Word List

fateful   throttle   caboose   locomotive
catwalk   cowcatcher   sandbox   right-of-way

1. Casey Jones was already famous when he went out on the <u>narrow, elevated platform</u> to save a little girl.

_____

2. He stepped on the <u>attachment at the front of the train</u> and scooped her up just before the train reached her.

_____

3. April 30, 1893, was <u>full of important consequences</u> for Casey Jones.

_____

4. In Vaughn, two cars and a <u>car at the rear of the train</u> were on the same track as Casey.

_____

5. They were blocking the <u>passageway that was Casey's right to use</u>.

_____

6. Casey pushed the <u>valve that controls the amount of power used</u> in to slow the engine.

_____

7. He also opened the <u>box full of sand</u> to snuff out the fire in the boiler.

_____

8. Casey's <u>engine that runs under its own power</u> crashed into the caboose, then leapt from the tracks, killing Casey.

_____

Write four or five complete sentences describing your feelings about what John Luther Jones did. Tell why you think he was a hero. Use a separate piece of paper.

Ghostly Tales

Whether or not you believe in ghosts, stories of ghostly visitations, hauntings, and unexplained activities can capture your imagination and give you shivers. Ghosts seem to find many different ways to attract attention. They may appear as occasional noises. There may be glimpses of ghostly figures. They cause assaults of sound, showers of stones, or mysterious movements of furniture or other household objects. There have been reports of items spontaneously catching fire. People have even claimed physical contact with ghosts that caused them harm. Some stories seem impossible to believe. However, one thing is clear. For those who have lived through such an experience, it has been life-altering.

There is a story told of a town in England. Loud, piercing noises assaulted the people for years. Then they stopped as suddenly and mysteriously as they had begun. Sometimes the noise took the form of a high-pitched hum, heard by many. At other times, a crushing pressure accompanied it. This affected individual people and caused them great pain and suffering before it stopped. The high-pitched whistle even stunned a flock of birds in mid-flight. They all fell to the ground, dead. Cats and dogs were affected by the noise as well, probably due to their fine hearing.

Many scientists and experts on ghostly activity have studied the area. They have tried to ascertain the cause for these disturbances. No one has ever come up with an explanation. As with most ghostly activity, it remains a mystery.

Go on to next page.

Directions

Answer each question about the story. Circle the letter in front of the correct answer.

1. What is the main idea of the story?
   a. Animals have finer hearing than people do.
   b. Most ghostly activity remains a mystery.
   c. England has many reports of ghosts.
   d. Ghost tales can be interesting to everyone.

2. Which of these is <u>not</u> mentioned in the story?
   a. Ghosts seem to find many different ways to attract attention.
   b. There have been reports of items spontaneously catching fire.
   c. Occasionally, ghostly activity has been proved a hoax.
   d. Many scientists and experts on ghostly activity have studied the area.

3. Where did the story of the unexplained noises take place?
   a. England
   b. France
   c. United States
   d. Canada

4. What happened to the flock of birds?
   a. They flew in a strange way.
   b. They lost their way.
   c. They lost their hearing.
   d. They were killed.

5. What would most likely make a person believe in ghosts?
   a. having a scientist explain their existence
   b. listening to someone who has had a ghostly encounter
   c. having a ghostly experience oneself
   d. watching a movie about a ghost

A Bit of Finn

It was a monstrous big river here, with the tallest and thickest kind of timber on both banks; just a solid wall, as well as I could see, by the stars. I looked away down stream, and seen a black speck on the water. I took out after it; but when I got to it it warn't nothing but a couple of saw-logs made fast together. Then I see another speck, and chased that; then another, and this time I was right. It was the raft.

When I got to it, Jim was sitting there with his head down between his knees, asleep, with his right arm hanging over the steering oar. The other oar was smashed off, and the raft was littered up with leaves and branches and dirt. So he'd had a rough time.

I made fast and laid down under Jim's nose on the raft, and begun to gap, and stretch my fists out against Jim and says:

"Hello, Jim, have I been asleep? Why didn't you stir me up?"

"Goodness gracious, is dat you, Huck? En you ain' dead—you ain' drownded—you's back agin? It's too good for true, honey, it's too good for true. Lemme look at you, chile, lemme feel o' you. No, you ain' dead! You's back agin, 'live en soun', jis de same ole Huck—de same ole Huck, thanks to goodness!"...

Jim said it made him all over trembly and feverish to be so close to freedom. Well, I can tell you it made me all over trembly and feverish, too, to hear him, because I begun to get it through my head that he was most free—and who was to blame for it? Why, me. I couldn't get that out of my conscience, no how or no way. It got to troubling me so I couldn't rest; I couldn't stay still in one place. It hadn't ever come home to me before, what this thing was that I was doing. But now it did; and it staid with me, and scorched me more and more. I tried to make out to myself that I warn't to blame, because I didn't run Jim off from his rightful owner; but it warn't no use, conscience up and says, every time, "But you knowed he was running for his freedom, and you could a paddled ashore and told somebody."

Unit II: A Tale to Tell

Improving Reading Comprehension 6, SV 5804-3

Directions

Read each sentence. Choose a word from the Word List that has the same meaning as the word or words in bold print. Write the word on the line.

Word List

conscience   feverish   scorched   rightful

1. Huck was feeling **greatly excited and bothered** thinking about how he had helped Jim.

_____

2. Huck's **knowledge of what is right and wrong** was bothering him. _____

3. Huck said that thinking of what he had done **burned** him more and more. _____

4. Huck had helped Jim escape from his **one who has lawful claim** owner. _____

Write *true* or *false* next to each sentence.

5. _____ Jim was in a boat on the river.

6. _____ Jim was asleep when Huck saw him.

7. _____ Huck pretended to be asleep on the raft.

8. _____ Huck was worried about having helped Jim escape.

9. _____ Huck would be in trouble if someone found he had helped Jim.

10. _____ Jim was not pleased to see Huck on the raft.

Huck has helped Jim escape from slavery to freedom. At the time, it was legal for a person to own slaves, and what Huck did was not legal. Write a paragraph describing why Huck is having conflicting emotions about helping Jim and whether or not you think he is doing the right thing.

_____

_____

_____

_____

_____

Tran's Secret

Tran could not believe that he was about to waste an evening. A group of his friends wanted him to join them for ghost stories around a campfire. At first, Tran had refused, saying, "Oh, that's stupid. Who wants to sit around listening to a bunch of stories that you know are made up, just to scare everyone? That stuff's for little kids!" Nevertheless, his friends had prevailed upon him to go. "Come on, Tran," they said. "It'll be fun."

So here he was, walking down this stupid path in these stupid woods so he could sit next to some stupid fire and listen to some stupid ghost stories! He glanced uneasily around him at the dark forms of the trees and listened to the croaking of the frogs. "Nothing scary in these woods," he said to himself. He took his place around the fire that had been built on the sand near the lake. Lisa began a story of a castle in England that had been haunted for years by the ghost  of a woman. In a soft voice meant to be spooky, Tran thought, Lisa related the tale. It was said that the woman had died of a broken heart. A man had been chosen for her to marry, but she had fallen in love with another man from the village. Her father did not approve, so he had had some of his hired hands kill the man from the village. When the girl found out, she had shut herself in one of the turrets of the castle and refused to eat or drink until she just wasted away.

A loon called out across the lake and sent shivers up Tran's spine. "Dumb bird," thought Tran. "I wish this story would end so we could get out of here."

"To this day," Lisa continued, "both the soft crying of the woman and the anguished wailing of her father can be heard in the castle. For when he found that his daughter was dead, the father was never the same again. He wandered around the castle and eventually went mad. One more thing— the door to the room that the girl died in cannot be opened easily. It has to be forced...and there is NOTHING to explain why." Just then, an owl hooted in a nearby tree, and Tran jumped up and screamed, causing everyone else to yell, too.

"Hey, Tran!" laughed Lisa. "I didn't scare you or anything, did I?"

"Me? Scared?" asked Tran. He looked around at the smiling faces of his friends. He was the only one standing, and he realized he was clutching his backpack tightly to his chest. So much for his big brave talk—now everyone knew he could be scared by a silly ghost story! He guessed the joke was on him. Slowly, he smiled. "Yeah, I guess I am scared!" he admitted. "Good story, Lisa."

Go on to next page.

Directions ————————————————————

Answer each question about the story. Circle the letter in front of the correct answer.

1. Tran's friends wanted him to _____.
   a. go camping with them
   b. listen to ghost stories
   c. swim in the lake
   d. build a campfire

2. Tran said he did not want to go because _____.
   a. it was for little kids
   b. it was too cold out
   c. he had something else to do
   d. he was afraid of the dark

3. In Lisa's story, who haunted the castle?
   a. a girl
   b. a man
   c. a girl and her father
   d. a girl and the man she loved

4. Tran said the loon was a "dumb bird" because _____.
   a. it was not intelligent
   b. it could not swim
   c. it flew near the fire
   d. it scared him

5. Tran had talked as if he could not be scared because _____.
   a. he did not want his friends to laugh at him
   b. he was not afraid of anything
   c. he did not know how to tell ghost stories
   d. he loved being in the dark woods

Telling Tales

Long before writing was invented, people told stories. These stories were an important way to pass on knowledge from one generation to the next and to entertain. Some stories were created to explain nature and the world. Myths were first told to explain the beginning of the world, the stars and planets, the weather, and human nature. Other tales were told about real people and happenings which were important at the time. These tales were told and retold through the years. Eventually, they became legends and their characters legendary, having greater strength, size, skill, and courage than any human being could possibly hope to equal. Before writing, storytellers were important members of society. Bards and singing minstrels wandered from town to town with tales to tell.

From short stories to novels, from poetry to epics and sagas, all are forms of literature. These are the ways in which stories have been written down. Although stories come in many forms, all stories have a plot, characters, theme, and a climax. The plot is the events as they unfold in the story. The characters are the people in the story who are affected by the happenings in the plot. A theme is the message that the author conveys through the characters and the plot. The climax is the part of the story when there is a turning point, or the most excitement.

It takes special talent to be a great storyteller, but storytelling is for everyone. Stories enrich our lives. We tell spooky stories around the campfire. We tell bedtime stories to put little ones to sleep. We tell tall tales to friends. However we use them, stories are fun, fascinating, and important to all of us.

Go on to next page.

Directions

Read each clue. Choose a word from the passage that best fits each clue. Write the words in the puzzle.

ACROSS

3. remarkable, extraordinary; famous
4. the telling of stories
7. singing, traveling storytellers
8. long stories of adventure and heroic deeds

DOWN

1. all imaginative writing in prose or verse
2. makes known
5. to give greater value to something
6. high point; turning point

Those Little Lies

When T.C. first told one of his friends that he had a cousin in Texas who was a champion rodeo rider, he had said it as a joke. Nevertheless, his friend Jake had been so impressed and excited by the news that T.C. had elaborated on it. Even then, he had every intention of coming clean and telling Jake that he was just kidding; but he was having too much fun. He gave the cousin a name, Travis Brady, and began telling about his cousin's accomplishments.

The next day, T.C. had forgotten all about Travis Brady, but Jake, apparently, had not. Soon T.C. had a group of classmates around him, eager for more news of this bronc-buster T.C. had for a cousin. It crossed T.C.'s mind at this point to tell everyone that he was only joking and that the cousin was purely fictional, but not only would T.C. be embarrassed to say so, Jake would be embarrassed as well. So the story got a little out of hand. Actually, the story got a lot out of hand. The kids were asking for pictures and news articles. They thought if Travis was so great, they surely would have seen him on television or read about him. T.C. began to feel uneasy about the story. He tried to think of a plan to get out of it.

Finally, after a few days of wrestling with his conscience, T.C. talked to Jake about the story. As he confessed, he noticed a big grin spreading across Jake's face. "What's so funny?" T.C. asked.

"You are, you dope," said Jake. "I knew your story was bogus, and so did everyone else. I saw your mom at my house later that day and asked her about it. She just laughed. Don't worry, though. I didn't tell her the whole thing, but that's why everyone was asking for so many details. I gotta say, you do spin a good tale; no one could get you to trip up!"

T.C. just stood there with his mouth hanging open—and not a word to say.

Directions ————————————————————————

Read each question about the story. Circle the letter in front of the correct answer.

1. When T.C. first told Jake about Travis, he was _____.
   a. perfectly serious
   b. only joking
   c. very upset
   d. talking in his sleep

2. Travis was supposed to be a _____ from Texas.
   a. rodeo clown
   b. bullfighter
   c. ranch hand
   d. rodeo rider

3. When T.C. went to school the next day, he found that _____.
   a. Jake had forgotten about the story
   b. Jake had shared the story with their friends
   c. Jake had asked his mother about the story
   d. Jake had figured out the story was not true

4. The word *fictional* means _____.
   a. real
   b. made up
   c. homemade
   d. in a book

5. Jake played the joke on T.C. because _____.
   a. he wanted T.C.'s mother to be angry at him
   b. he owed T.C. for a joke T.C. had played on him once
   c. he wanted to teach T.C. a lesson
   d. he did not want T.C. for a friend any longer

Stealing Home

Mohamed was learning to speak and understand English quickly, although he had only been in Indiana three weeks, and he still had a lot to learn. He had never played baseball before, but he was really happy that his new friends had asked him to play.

The Spiders were at bat first. They had two players on bases when Mohamed came to bat. "Swing, batter!" the pitcher yelled as he threw the first pitch. Mohamed began to swing his hips and looked over at Mike Mahoney to see if he was doing it right. "Stee—rike!" called the umpire.

The next pitch was wild. "Ball!" called the umpire.

"Yes, yes," Mohamed remarked, smiling and pointing to the catcher picking it up. "The ball is over there."

"Get him out of there!" Coach Miller groaned. But just then Mohamed whacked the third pitch far out to left field. Within seconds, Mohamed had driven in two runs and was on third base himself.

Mike quickly ran over to give Mohamed some coaching. "Now," he said, "the next time the catcher has to run after a wild pitch, steal home plate. Do you understand?" Mohamed smiled broadly and nodded.

The very next pitch was wild. "Go for it!" Mike yelled. "Steal! Steal! Run for home!" Mohamed raced to home plate, yanked the base out of the ground, and ran out of the park with it. He could hear everyone screaming behind him, and he was very happy.

Go on to next page.

Directions

Answer each question about the story. Circle the letter in front of the correct answer.

1. Mohamed has trouble with some of the meanings of words used in baseball because _____.
   a. he has never heard English before
   b. the other players aren't speaking English
   c. he is just learning English and the special language of baseball
   d. the players don't speak very clearly

2. When Mohamed hears the pitcher yell "Swing, batter!" he thinks he is supposed to _____.
   a. swing his body
   b. strike out
   c. run to a swing in the park
   d. strike the umpire

3. When the umpire calls "Ball," Mohamed thinks the umpire is _____.
   a. saying that the pitch was bad
   b. trying to locate the ball
   c. saying that Mohamed was "out"
   d. telling the pitcher to throw the ball

4. One word that confuses Mohamed and that causes him to take home plate away with him is _____.
   a. *understand*
   b. *now*
   c. *steal*
   d. *wild*

5. As Mohamed leaves the park, he thinks the other players are yelling because _____.
   a. they are angry at him
   b. they want him to bring back home plate
   c. he is running in the wrong direction
   d. he had played the game so well

It's How You Look at It

Everybody knew that Jake's father collected junk. Well, it looked like junk, anyway. When you drove by their house, you could see all that old stuff out back in the weeds, and their garage was one huge junk warehouse. Jake was quiet at school, and he didn't bring friends home. No one had any real complaints about Jake, but no one knew him well, either, so he never quite seemed to fit in. The other students didn't go out of their way to get better acquainted with Jake. He must be strange—what kind of people would collect all that junk?

One day Jake's class was assigned a task in science. They were put into groups and told to create a space vehicle out of scraps, trash, and other found objects. They were instructed not to spend any money on their project. Grading was to be done on imagination and ingenuity.

While most of the class was wondering where on Earth they would find these objects, Jake's mind immediately set to cataloguing what his father had stored in his garage and in the backyard. He could picture some great possibilities. He figured he probably had enough stuff to make ten space vehicles! He knew his dad wouldn't mind, either. He would say what he always said, "Hey, that's what the stuff is for. Help yourself!"

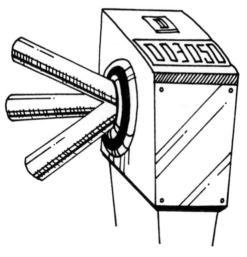

As the days went by, the rest of the groups began to hear about what was happening in Jake's group. While the rest of the class expressed their admiration for the plans Jake's group had drawn up, Jake suddenly realized that he had taken all his resources for granted. These other kids didn't have half the stuff his group had at its disposal. He shyly offered the whole class an opportunity to come to his house and take whatever they wanted. Everyone was appreciative of Jake and his father's generosity. Suddenly, Jake's yard and garage seemed to be filled with treasure instead of junk, and the whole class built such interesting vehicles that they were prominently displayed for the rest of the year.

Go on to next page.

Name_____   Date_____

Directions

Read each clue. Choose a word from the story that best fits each clue. Write the words in the puzzle.

ACROSS

2. for you to use, or dispose of
4. grateful
7. got to know; became familiar with
8. things that one can use

DOWN

1. organizing; ordering
3. creative thinking; cleverness
5. standing out; easy to see
6. used for carrying people and goods from one place to another

A Stray to Stay

The first time I saw him, he was lying on the porch. He held his shoulders and head high, and despite the fact that his coat was not groomed, he made it clear that he had a high opinion of himself.

I expected him to run as I came up the steps, but instead, he moved only his head, the bright yellow eyes following me. He acted as though he owned the place.

He was still out there that afternoon and was there, lying in the sun, the next morning. He purred, and I decided it was safe to pet him. I could tell he was a stray. Some college students around here get pets and then just go off and leave them when it's time to go home for the summer. "OK," I thought, "you can stay." As if I had anything to say about it. I brought him some food and water, and he gulped it down and then sauntered off. I felt used.

That afternoon I saw him by the steps of a house three doors down. "The nerve of him!" I thought. "See here," I said, walking up some steps toward him. "You had better make up your mind where you are going to live—here or with me." I was very sincere about feeling rejected, and I realized I had come to like him. My voice showed it.

When I got home, he was on my porch again. He's been there—when he's not inside—ever since. We both consider this to be "our place."

Directions

Answer each question about the story. Circle the letter in front of the correct answer.

1. The cat is on the writer's porch because he _____.
   a. had decided to lie there
   b. is hiding from some students
   c. had been raised by the writer
   d. had just finished dinner

2. One detail suggesting that the cat is a stray is that _____.
   a. he acts as though he were lost
   b. he has a high opinion of himself
   c. his coat needs grooming
   d. he acts right at home

3. After the writer first feeds the cat, the cat _____.
   a. lies in the sun and takes a nap
   b. saunters off to go somewhere else
   c. disappears for several days
   d. sits at his door begging for more food

4. When the writer sees the cat on the neighbor's porch, he feels _____.
   a. relieved that the cat has found someone else
   b. as though the cat has rejected him
   c. sorry that he had chased it away
   d. happy to know that it is not a stray

5. The writer speaks firmly to the cat because he _____.
   a. wants the cat to go away
   b. knows the cat belongs to someone else
   c. has nothing to feed the cat
   d. hopes the cat will live with him and not the neighbor

A Good Guide

Darla Kemp's younger brother, Paul, was not like other boys his age. Instead of hanging around with all the other kids after school and on weekends, he would disappear into the woods or along the backroads of town, rambling along and picking up anything he found that seemed interesting. He had a fascinating collection of arrowheads and antique square nails; he had whole birds' nests with the eggs still in them, found abandoned on the ground. He could identify most birdcalls and all the wildflowers he encountered in his travels. Still, he was friendly enough in spite of his differences. He enjoyed the company of other people and was even fun to be with. He had a great sense of humor and was always willing to help. That was why, when Darla and two of her friends went backpacking, they let Paul accompany them.

Paul kept quiet most of the time, bringing up the rear of the line. He seemed absorbed in his own thoughts, while the girls kept up their own chatter and took whatever path presented itself. They had no real destination planned; they were hoping to see something new, maybe find a new place they would want to revisit later.

Around noon, they climbed out on some rocks overhanging a stream and emptied their packs for lunch. Eventually, they decided that it was probably about time to head back home, but they could not agree on which way to go. They had found a new place, that was true, but they also seemed to be lost! They discussed at length what they should do and tried to remember all the signs to tell them which way was north and south. The girls found that their collective knowledge of the woods was not very impressive.

"Great," said Darla with a sigh. "I'm going to get in trouble for taking my little brother into the woods and getting him lost!"

"I'm not lost," Paul spoke up as he calmly finished his cookies and stowed his trash in his pack. "I've been here plenty of times."

"Paul!" exclaimed Darla. "Why didn't you say something? We've been trying to decide how to get home for the last half hour!"

"Well, I guess because no one asked," he said. "I haven't been listening all that much."

Darla looked at her friends and shrugged. "Who knew?" she said. "All this time we had our own private guide, and we were worried about being lost!"

Go on to next page.

Name_____   Date_____

Directions _____

Rewrite each sentence. Use a word with the same meaning from the Word List in place of the underlined words.

Word List
destination   overhanging   rambling   encountered

1. Paul often went <u>for long, aimless strolls</u> through the woods around his town.

_____

2. He brought home many of the interesting items that he <u>met up with</u> on his journeys.

_____

3. The girls had no particular <u>place to stop or end</u> to their walk.

_____

4. They stopped and ate lunch on some rocks <u>hanging out over</u> a stream.

_____

Choose the word that best fits each sentence. Write the word in the blank.

5. Paul liked to travel along the_____ of the town as well as through the woods.
   background   backroads   backpacks

6. Darla and her friends went _____ together.
   backing   climbing   backpacking

7. They were hoping to find a place that they could _____.
   revisit   relive   restore

8. When it was time to leave, they discovered that their _____ knowledge of the woods did not amount to much.
   collected   collection   collective

Looking for Trouble

"Who is it you'll be with today
when you go down to the park to play?
What's his name?" I heard Father say.

"Yeah, whatshisname. You know. That guy."
When I talk to Dad I never lie.
I wouldn't even want to try.

"Did you say Billy Beanalee?"
Now Dad was looking straight at me,
and I nodded yes. "Oh, no! not he!"

"Not that rascal!" Father said.
"You'll come home injured, or, worse yet, dead!"
He was holding and shaking his head.

"He's not a good influence, that boy!
There's not a soul he can't annoy,"
Dad said. "He's too clever, and he's coy!"

So I left my father in a worried way
and went off to join my friend in play.
I was late, and Billy had come halfway.

"I bet they lectured you back there,"
he said. "But gosh, it isn't fair
that I get more trouble than my share."

"Let's just sit," he said. "Not do a thing
and hope that my luck doesn't bring
us trouble . . . or boredom . . . or anything."

He twiddled his thumbs, gave a yawn or two,
then said, "I'll tell you what we'll do.
I'll find trouble and run it off for you!"

Go on to next page.

Directions

Answer each question about the poem. Circle the letter in front of the correct answer.

1. Father thinks that Billy is _____.
   a. a clever boy who has bad luck
   b. a boy who worries too much
   c. someone who will protect his son
   d. a bad influence on his son

2. The boy who is telling the story tries to avoid lying to his father by _____.
   a. acting as though he doesn't hear him
   b. talking about something else
   c. calling Billy "whatshisname"
   d. asking a question himself

3. Billy thinks his friend is late because his _____.
   a. friend doesn't really want to come
   b. friend's parents didn't want him to play with Billy
   c. friend didn't know how to find the park
   d. friend had got in trouble somewhere on the way to the park

4. Billy thinks the reason he gets in trouble so often is that _____.
   a. his friends are troublemakers
   b. everyone expects it of him
   c. life is unfair to him
   d. he sits and lets it find him

5. The end of the poem tells the reader that Billy is the kind of person who _____.
   a. goes looking for trouble
   b. really does have bad luck
   c. tries to stay out of trouble
   d. tries to make his friend's parents like him

A World of Difference

"It takes all kinds." This phrase, or saying, can be used in different ways to mean different things. Sometimes, people will say it in bewilderment when they don't understand other people's actions. Sometimes, it will be said in a ridiculing way, to make fun of someone who is different from the speaker. A broader interpretation of the phrase, however, is one that holds much meaning for all of us.

Can you imagine what the world would be like if we were all the same? People's differences, or our diversity, is what makes our lives work. Because there are people who like to look for reasons in science, we have scientific discoveries and medical breakthroughs. Because there are those who watch the world with a writer's mind, we have countless books to read and enjoy. Because there are people who are born with other talents, like artists, photographers, architects, and designers of all kinds, we are given choices in everything. Some of us want to lead; others want to follow. Some people like crowds; others prefer to be alone. There is no end to our differences.

People are diverse inside and out. Because of the many different cultures that surround us, there is always something new for us to learn about or experience in food, dress, and other customs.

Sometimes it takes growing older to discover just what you want to be or do. As you get older, it gets easier to express your individuality. It can be difficult to be different when you are young. Peer pressures on young people to be just alike can be strong. As you get older, you will begin to find your niche and be less concerned about what everyone else thinks. Then the real, special, and diverse you can stand up, and you can express yourself in your own unique way.

Go on to next page.

Name_____ Date_____

Directions

Think about the passage you read. Then fill in the blanks of the following paragraph with words from the Word List.

Word List

ridiculing   individuality   niche   diversity
bewilderment   breakthroughs   peer   interpretation

The phrase, "It takes all kinds," can be said in a **1)** _____ way, putting

someone down who is different. It may also be said in **2)** _____, when someone

does not understand another person. A broader **3)** _____, or meaning, refers to

our differences, or our **4)** _____. Because people are different and express their

5) _____ in different ways, we have some people who become artists and

others who help bring about medical **6)** _____. When people are young,

7) _____ pressure can make expressing one's individuality difficult. As we get

older, we begin to find our **8)** _____.

Write *fact* or *opinion* in front of each sentence.

9. _____ Older people find it easier to express their individuality.

10. _____ There is much peer pressure on young people to be alike.

11. _____ Peer pressure is difficult to deal with.

12. _____ Some people like to lead; others prefer to follow.

13. _____ It is not fair to ridicule people who are different from yourself.

14. _____ Because of the many different cultures in the world, we can try new

foods and learn about new customs.

15. _____ The world would be boring if we were all the same.

Babysitting Blues

Babysitting with the Jordan children is a real challenge. Sharon Kling took the job one afternoon when Mrs. Jordan went out. Little Biff soon dropped some crackers on the floor on purpose and then danced on top of them, crying, "I'm sorry!"

Pamela, the oldest, told Sharon that the vacuum cleaner was at the back of a big hall closet. While Sharon was in there searching, the children locked her in. Although they let her out before their mother came home, Sharon never sat for them again.

One time they surrounded Bobby Winters from the rear, tied him up, and danced war dances around him for an hour.

Corky Duncan took the job once last winter. The furnace went off, so he took the Jordan children to his house to stay warm. Then his dad went to check the Jordan's furnace to keep their water pipes from freezing.

"Someone turned the thermostat down as far as it would go," Mr. Duncan said when he got back. "Then someone took the knob off and put it back to look as if it were set at 75."

Corky looked down at the four angel faces smiling and stuffing cookies into their mouths. "Aren't those the cookies the mice were nibbling on last week?" he asked his mother.

"Yes," she replied, winking, "but only *good* children get to eat the fresh, clean ones!"

Go on to next page.

Directions

Answer each question about the selection. Circle the letter in front of the correct answer.

1. Sharon Kling goes into the Jordan hall closet to _____.
   a. look for Pamela
   b. get the vacuum cleaner
   c. get Biff out of there
   d. look for a key

2. Sharon never sits for the Jordans a second time because she _____.
   a. is always busy
   b. had been locked in a closet
   c. does not like checking the furnace
   d. does not enjoy war dances

3. The Jordan children once tied up _____.
   a. Corky Duncan
   b. Sharon Kling
   c. Mr. Duncan
   d. Bobby Winters

4. Corky thinks that the thermostat at the Jordan house _____.
   a. has been chewed by mice
   b. has been turned way down
   c. is set at 75 degrees
   d. has a missing knob

5. Corky teases about the cookies because he _____.
   a. can't fix the Jordan furnace
   b. wants to save them for himself
   c. wants to get back at the children just a little
   d. is angry with his mother

Hector the Hero

"I don't like sitting next to Hector," Sally complained. "He doesn't have any feelings."

"Probably not," Lil said. "Hector's an android."

"He buzzes and squeaks when he moves," Sally said, "and he eats synch pudding for lunch! I don't see what he's doing in school. They could program him to know everything that they want a machine to know."

"It's an experiment," Lil said. "They want to know if he can learn new things if they start him out with only the basic program."

That afternoon there was a sudden blizzard. No one could get out of the school, and the electricity and furnace went off. "I'm freezing!" Sally cried. Then the principal called Hector out of the room, and soon Sally could feel the heat was back on.

"Hector's down in the basement," Lil explained. "He's transferring his energy to the furnace to keep it running. They're carrying synch pudding to him by the bucketful. Want to help by taking him some?"

The girls found Hector standing with his hand on the big motor. He looked at Sally with pale gray eyes, and she could see that he was getting very weak.

"He can't last long," Lil whispered to Sally.

Soon the lights came back on. A helicopter brought food and blankets, and some people carried Hector away on a stretcher. "They're taking him back to the factory that made him," Lil said. As he came past Sally, Hector just managed to raise one hand. He smiled a weak smile and waved a small good-bye.

"Oh," Sally said, her eyes filling with tears, "he does have feelings. I hope that they fix him quickly."

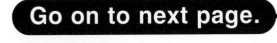
Go on to next page.

Directions

Answer each question about the story. Circle the letter in front of the correct answer.

1. Sally doesn't like Hector at first because he _____.
   a. doesn't have enough energy
   b. works in a factory
   c. is sloppy when he eats
   d. isn't like everyone else

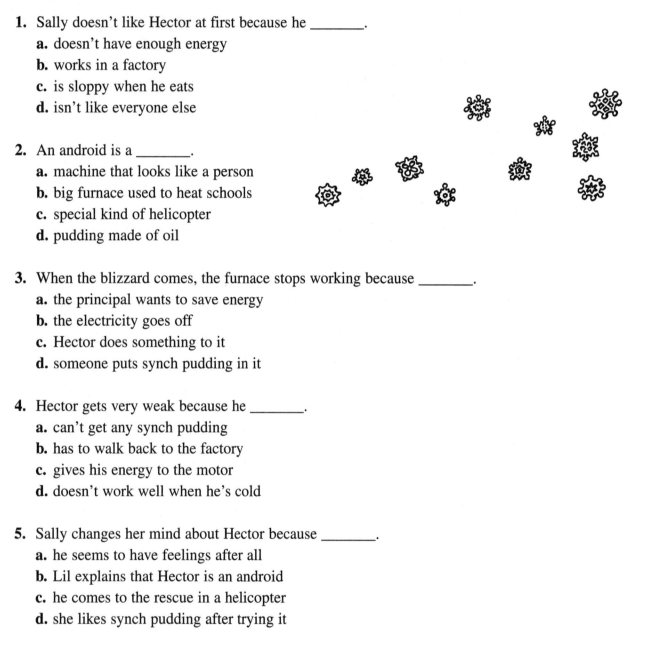

2. An android is a _____.
   a. machine that looks like a person
   b. big furnace used to heat schools
   c. special kind of helicopter
   d. pudding made of oil

3. When the blizzard comes, the furnace stops working because _____.
   a. the principal wants to save energy
   b. the electricity goes off
   c. Hector does something to it
   d. someone puts synch pudding in it

4. Hector gets very weak because he _____.
   a. can't get any synch pudding
   b. has to walk back to the factory
   c. gives his energy to the motor
   d. doesn't work well when he's cold

5. Sally changes her mind about Hector because _____.
   a. he seems to have feelings after all
   b. Lil explains that Hector is an android
   c. he comes to the rescue in a helicopter
   d. she likes synch pudding after trying it

Never Say Never

Peter was walking in the mall when he heard a woman yelling at her son. "Come on!" she said, irritably. "Keep up with me and stop fooling around!" She took the boy's hand and pulled him along, looking very angry and exasperated. "Gee," thought Peter. "What a grouch that woman is. I would never yell at a little kid like that, especially when he wasn't even doing anything!"

A few days later, Peter was babysitting his nephew, Brock, for the afternoon when he decided to go for a walk and pick up a few things that he needed downtown at the same time. Peter had watched his nephew before, and he knew he had his work cut out keeping Brock entertained all afternoon; maybe the walk would keep him occupied for an hour or so.

In the music store, Peter purchased some guitar strings. While Peter was at the register, Brock almost knocked over a whole rack of expensive guitars. Peter grabbed his nephew just in time to save them. "That was close," he thought. His next stop was a sports shop where he wanted to check on a card he needed for his collection. He didn't have time to look for the card, though, because Brock began jumping in and out of the clothes racks. Then he bumped into a row of bats and knocked them all asunder. Peter made Brock help him straighten the bats and then got out of the store quickly. Peter had just one more thing he wanted to accomplish, but he wasn't sure he should attempt it with Brock in tow. Nevertheless, they entered the discount store, and Peter found a new pair of laces for his sneakers. He grasped Brock's hand the entire time so that Brock would stay out of trouble, but when they got out of the store and halfway home, Peter discovered that Brock had a package of caramels clenched in his hand.

"Brock!" Peter yelled. "This is bad! Now we have to go all the way back to the store to return these!" Peter was holding the caramels, pointing at a crestfallen Brock, whose lower lip was stuck out and trembling, when suddenly he had a recollection of the woman in the mall. "Oh, well," he thought with a sigh. "Never say never, right? Maybe she was having the worst day imaginable, too!"

"Come on. Let's return these, or better yet, pay for them," he said to Brock, looking at the somewhat squashed candy. "And then we'll get an ice cream, all right?"

"Ice cream!" Brock yelled enthusiastically. "Chocolate ice cream with sprinkles."

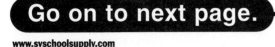

Name_____   Date_____

Directions

Choose the word that best fits each sentence. Write the word in the blank.

1. The woman Peter saw had spoken _____ to her son.

   irregularly   irritably   happily

2. She was clearly _____.

   excited   exasperated   young

3. Brock knocked _____ a row of bats.

   asunder   under   with

4. Peter bought his shoelaces at a _____ store.

   drug   distant   discount

5. When Peter yelled at Brock, Brock looked _____.

   pleased   creased   crestfallen

6. Peter suddenly had a _____ of the woman at the mall.

   recalled   picture   recollection

7. He decided that perhaps she had had the worst day _____, too.

   imagination   shopping   imaginable

8. When Peter suggested ice cream, Brock responded _____.

   enthusiastically   sadly   carelessly

Write *true* or *false* next to each sentence.

9. _____ Peter had cared for his nephew on previous occasions.

10. _____ Peter's nephew was easy to watch.

11. _____ Brock knocked over a glove display.

12. _____ Peter had to pay for a damaged guitar.

13. _____ Peter became frustrated when he saw the candy in Brock's hand.

14. _____ Peter realized that he had probably judged the woman in the mall unfairly.

15. _____ Peter and Brock returned to the store with the candy.

16. _____ Brock did not care for ice cream.

Time Travel

What happens to you when you travel through time?
Do you lose your balance or forget how to rhyme?
Do you float through the sky not knowing where
Or when will be now when here is there?

Why do so many insist on unraveling
This mystery about time traveling?
If we threw away calendars, clocks,
Watches, and all that tick-tocks,

If about time we never did hear,
In a moment, a flash, or just
In a flicker of a ticker,
Would everything and

everyone suddenly
Just dis
app
ea
r
?

Directions

Answer each question about the poem. Circle the letter in front of the correct answer.

1. What is the purpose of the poem?
   a. to explain how to travel through time
   b. to raise questions about time travel
   c. to make fun of people who believe in time travel
   d. to encourage people to try time travel

2. What does the poem say might happen without time?
   a. Everything and everyone might disappear.
   b. Everyone will be late for meetings.
   c. No one will know what to do.
   d. Night and day will become the same.

3. What does the poem say so many insist on unraveling?
   a. the mysteries of the world
   b. the mysteries of science
   c. the reason time traveling makes you lose your balance
   d. the mystery about time traveling

Answer each question about the poem.

4. What does the shape of the poem have to do with what the poem is saying?

   _____

   _____

   _____

5. Write a poem of your own. Make its shape connect to your poem's message in some way. Use another sheet of paper if you need more room.

One More Night

The tent was up, and inside it, the sleeping bags were spread out on foam pads. The cooler was full of good things to eat, and a fire was all set for when they returned from their walk in the forest. It was a nice spot, surrounded by tall pines and hardwoods. The forest floor was covered with soft pine needles and leaves, and the scent of pine and balsam floated on the air. Bailey knew she should be appreciative of this chance to be here with her dad in the woods, but she could not seem to relax. He had been planning this weekend for months, but she had been dreading it for just as long.

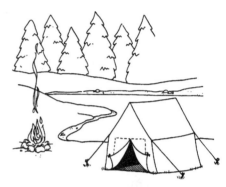

Bailey liked being in her own house, sleeping in her own bed, cleaning up in her bathroom where there was hot running water, and eating bug-free at the kitchen table. Here, she would have to clean up in a river in which lived all manner of fish and other disagreeable water creatures, sleep in a tent in the dark in the middle of nowhere, and eat with the bugs. They would have to cook their own food over a campfire and wash the dishes in the river. It all seemed like too much work to Bailey, and the woods were scary, too. She tried not to betray her real feelings to her father; she didn't want to disappoint him, but this seemed like a nightmare!

Bailey and her father went for a walk before supper. It was very quiet in the woods, and their feet hardly made a sound on the soft carpet of needles. They saw a beaver that slapped its tail on the water and then dove underneath, leaving barely a ripple on the surface. They later saw him climb up the embankment on the far side of the river and disappear into the woods. They saw chipmunks and rabbits. A fox streaked by farther up the path. Boisterous jays scolded them for walking too near.

That evening after dinner, the sky was dotted with millions of shining stars. As the fire burned down to embers, the soft lapping of the water on the shore and the sound of the creatures in the woods were more comforting than ominous, as Bailey had expected. Her sleeping bag was soft and warm, and she woke to the sound of birds singing and the smell of bacon frying. In the fresh, early-morning air, she splashed her face with the clear river water. Today they were planning to break camp and head for home. She looked over at her father, cracking eggs into the frying pan and humming to himself. He seemed to be having fun; maybe she could convince him to stay for one more night.

Go on to next page.

Directions

Read each clue. Choose a word from the story that best fits each clue. Write the words in the puzzle.

ACROSS

2. coals
4. grateful
7. a time early in the day
8. frightening; threatening

DOWN

1. unpleasant
3. noisy and lively
5. wall of earth
6. kinds of trees; tough, heavy wood

Alyson's Wish

Uncle Will bought the necklace from an old woman, who said that it had magic power. She refused to tell how to use the power. "It's a bad thing," she said.

Alyson held her gift from Uncle Will to the light. Its stone cast an orange beam into the room. "If I believe that, I can rub the stone and make a wish that will come true." She wished for sunshine, but didn't get it.

Alyson had an idea. She would tell her little sister, Clara, that this was a magic necklace. Clara would believe her. Then two would believe—three, if she counted the old lady; then the magic would work.

Clara asked what Alyson was wishing for as her big sister rubbed the stone before they got in bed. "I wish every week had only Saturdays," Alyson said.

When they got up the next morning, it was Saturday. "But it was Sunday yesterday," Clara said.

"I know," Alyson said, jumping with glee.

Weeks later, Alyson sat on her bed one morning. "It's Saturday again," she said, yawning. "I'm so tired of Saturdays. I wish I could go to school." She began rubbing the stone and wishing for Monday.

Clara awakened and heard her. "It's no use," Clara said. "I knew from the beginning that it only gives one wish to each person." The girls looked at each other and smiled. Slowly Alyson handed Clara the necklace so that Clara could make her wish.

Soon their mother was at the door. "Time to get ready for school, girls," she said.

"I will never give this necklace to anyone else," Alyson said. "People are too careless with wishes."

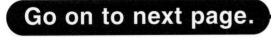

Go on to next page.

Directions

Answer each question about the selection. Circle the letter in front of the correct answer.

1. Alyson believes that the necklace will work if _____.
   a. enough people believe it will
   b. she gets Clara to make the wishes
   c. she finds the right spot to rub
   d. she gets the light to shine through it

2. Alyson wishes for _____.
   a. another necklace
   b. a gift from Uncle Will
   c. weeks made up of Saturdays
   d. a chance to talk to the old woman

3. Soon after Alyson gets her wish, she feels that _____.
   a. she should begin wishing for other things
   b. a life of Saturdays is wonderful
   c. the necklace's power is not a bad thing
   d. having nothing but Saturdays is boring

4. Clara realizes that the necklace would _____.
   a. never grant her a wish
   b. change colors when it was rubbed
   c. only give one wish to each person
   d. only work for a short while

5. When Clara's wish comes true, she probably feels _____.
   a. surprised and angry
   b. upset and fearful
   c. happy but anxious
   d. relieved and satisfied

Little Louisa

Carmen knew that she should be happy for her aunt because her aunt was going to have a baby. Carmen's Aunt Sonya and Uncle Carl had wanted a baby for many years, so many years they had almost come to accept the fact that they would never have children. Now they were going to have a child, and they were ecstatic. So was everyone else, it seemed. Carmen loved to see her Aunt Sonya so happy, but there was a part of Carmen that could not appreciate the arrival of a new baby.

For years, Carmen had been able to escape from her own large family of six children and run to her Aunt Sonya's. Whenever she felt the urge to get away from the noise and the arguing, the

teasing and the general craziness of her big household, there was Aunt Sonya, calm, quiet, and always pleased to see Carmen. They would spend hours together talking, walking, doing each other's nails, shopping, watching movies, or just reading quietly. Carmen cherished her time with Aunt Sonya. She believed that once the baby came and Aunt Sonya had someone of her own, she would not have the time or the inclination to spend time with Carmen. Carmen saw the new baby as an intrusion. She didn't see how things could ever be the same.

Of course, when Louisa was born, things never were the same. Nevertheless, things were wonderful. Carmen should have known that her Aunt Sonya would have a way of including Carmen in everything. Sonya still wanted Carmen to come over all the time. Together, they dressed and bathed little Louisa. As Louisa got older, Carmen helped with feeding and spent many hours playing with her new niece. It was not quite as quiet at Aunt Sonya's as it once was, but Carmen's time with her aunt and Louisa had a special new quality all its own.

Go on to next page.

Name _____   Date _____

Directions

Read each sentence. Choose a word from the Word List that has the same meaning as the word or words in bold print. Write the word on the line.

Word List
inclination   cherished   craziness   ecstatic   intrusion

1. To Carmen, the baby was an **unwelcome thing forced upon her**. _____

2. Carmen **held in high regard** her quiet times with her Aunt Sonya. _____

3. Carmen liked to go to her aunt's house to escape the **wildness** of her own. _____

4. Carmen did not think that her aunt would have the **leaning toward; desire** to spend time with her once the baby was born. _____

5. Aunt Sonya and Uncle Carl were **incredibly happy** about the new baby. _____

Write *true* or *false* next to each sentence.

6. _____ Carmen's family was large and noisy.

7. _____ Carmen did not like babies.

8. _____ Sonya had waited a long time to have a baby.

9. _____ Carmen was afraid that Sonya would not have time for her.

10. _____ Sonya included Carmen in the care of the new baby.

11. _____ Carmen loved her new niece.

Another Person's Shoes

You will experience, many times in your life, lessons that teach you not to judge a person's actions or a situation until you have all the facts. Judging things just from appearances can cause embarrassment. It can be unfair to the person who is judged. There are many old sayings that suggest that we should not rush our judgments, such as "Don't judge a book by its cover," and "Don't judge a person until you have walked a mile in his or her shoes." A person might say, "Well, what would *you* do if you were in *my* shoes?" All these things mean that before you say what you would do, or what you think someone else should have done in a situation, you should consider all of the circumstances.

Often you will hear young people say that they will never do the things that their parents do. Sometimes this turns out to be true; but another very common comment by people who become parents is that they have found themselves doing just those things that they said they would not do when they were younger. Why have they changed? It is because as young people with no children, they could not understand what makes parents act the way they do. Once a person becomes a parent, it often becomes clear what caused their own parents to make the decisions that they made. The new parents are actually "walking in the shoes" of their own parents. Now they understand!

Before you judge another person or say what you would *never* do, put yourself in the other person's position. Think of all of the factors. It may be that we can never fully understand another person's motives, but we can try. So many things affect a person's decision that the decision made one day may not even be the same one that would be made the next day or the next week. Financial pressures, social pressures, stress at home or at work, and even the weather can be factors in decision-making. This is not to say that there is always an excuse for a bad decision, just that all decisions that *seem* bad may not *be* bad. They may have been the best choice available at the time.

The next time you question someone's actions, think whatever you like. But before you pass judgment aloud, be sure you have thought long enough about what is fair.

Go on to next page.

Directions

Answer each question about the passage. Circle the letter in front of the correct answer.

1. What is the author's purpose in this passage?
   a. to explain why we cannot make judgments about other people
   b. to describe the correct way to make a decision
   c. to tell how to try on other people's shoes
   d. to warn against quick judgments of other people

2. What does the author say is important to consider?
   a. the other person's shoe size
   b. all the factors that affect a person's decision
   c. what the weather is like
   d. whether or not the person has children

3. Which saying is similar to part of the author's message?
   a. An ounce of medicine is worth a pound of cure.
   b. Beauty is in the eye of the beholder.
   c. He who laughs last, laughs best.
   d. Never say never.

4. The word *financial* refers to _____.
   a. money
   b. family
   c. employment
   d. friends

5. Which of these is <u>not</u> mentioned as a factor in decision-making?
   a. age
   b. financial pressures
   c. social pressures
   d. the weather

Name_____   Date_____

Rhino's Return

Everyone in town knew the rhinoceros. It sat in front of the small gallery for almost fifteen years. People forgot that it was for sale, probably because they thought it was too heavy to move. It was sculpted from limestone and weighed tons.

People would lean on the rhino and run their hands over its smooth back. Fathers would lift their children up to sit on the sculpture's broad back. Everyone loved the rhinoceros, and it had become a landmark and part of the landscape near the gallery.

When a big flatbed truck and crane came to lift it and take it away, everyone was startled! The man who made it had it moved to his new home many miles away.

Many people were angry, but the students in one school thought about it carefully. They understood that the sculpture was for sale. Until someone bought it, it belonged to the sculptor; and he could haul it anywhere he pleased. The students began a campaign to raise $6,000 to buy it so they could bring it back and put it in the playground at their school. They held a benefit carnival. They made things to sell. The sculptor even made a small stone rhino, and the children sold tickets to raffle it off.

Before long, the class had raised $4,000; and it looked as though they would be able one day to buy the rhino and bring it back home to their town.

Go on to next page.

Directions

Answer each question about the story. Circle the letter in front of the correct answer.

1. Before the sculptor moves it, the rhino is _____.
   a. in a zoo in a city nearby
   b. on the school playground
   c. at the sculptor's house
   d. in front of a small gallery

2. People take the huge rhinoceros for granted because _____.
   a. it has been in their town a long time
   b. they never paid any attention to it
   c. it is made of stone and not real
   d. the sculptor had given it to the gallery

3. The money raised by raffling off the small rhino goes to _____.
   a. move the sculpture to the sculptor's home
   b. pay the expenses for the carnival
   c. help the students raise money
   d. build a playground for the school

4. When the sculptor learns that the children want to buy the large rhino, he probably feels _____.
   a. sad to part with it after so long
   b. happy that they appreciate it
   c. annoyed that they want it back again
   d. upset because the gallery owner did not buy it

5. Until someone buys it for $6,000, the huge rhino belongs to the _____.
   a. school
   b. children
   c. sculptor
   d. gallery

Tracking Tess

Karen's little sister, Tess, could be so troublesome and annoying, sometimes Karen just wanted her to get lost. Now, however, Tess really was lost; and Karen would have given anything just to see her little sister's face and hear her voice!

Apparently, Tess had wandered away from the house in the morning while her mother was cleaning. When her mother interrupted her vacuuming to check on Tess, she was gone. After searching the entire house and yard, and calling repeatedly for Tess, Karen's mother frantically called Karen at her friend's house. Her mother, worried to distraction, told her to come right home and help look for Tess.

Karen pondered where her sister would have gone. At first, she could come up with no ideas that hadn't already been checked. Then she began to think like Tess. Maybe if she tried to think of things the way Tess did, she could figure out where she had gone. She tried to remember things she and Tess talked about and suddenly recalled Tess's preoccupation with the swans at the lake. Karen and Tess had seen the swans a couple of weeks before, and Tess had been persistently asking Karen to take her back ever since. Karen told her mother she had an idea and jumped on her bike, pedaling as fast as she could toward the lake. Karen could hardly conceive of little Tess wandering this far from the house, but Karen had to check out every possibility.

When Karen arrived at the lake, she tossed her bike aside and began calling to Tess. She ran to the spot where they had last seen the swans. She was elated to see Tess, sitting very quietly and looking at Karen, with her finger to her lips. "Shhh," she whispered. "Babies!" Karen moved to Tess's side and looked over the lake. There were the two adult swans, and now two little cygnets paddled along after them. Karen watched them for a moment, admiring the elegance of the older swans, and then remembered her poor mother. She gave her sister a hug and said, "Boy, am I glad to see you! Come on now, we've got to get you home. Mom will be happy to see you, too!"

Go on to next page.

Name_____   Date_____

Directions

Think about the passage you read. Then fill in the blanks of the following paragraph with words from the Word List.

Word List

pondered   preoccupation   cygnets   elegance
elated   persistently   conceive   distraction

When Karen's mother couldn't find Tess, she was worried to **1)** _____. Karen

2) _____ the question of where her sister could have gone, and she remembered that

Tess had **3)** _____ asked her to go back to the lake to see the swans. She seemed to

have a **4)** _____ with those birds. It seemed impossible to **5)** _____

that Tess could have gotten all the way to the lake, but Karen had to check. Karen was

6) _____ to find Tess at the lake. She saw that there were now two young

7) _____ with the older swans. Karen admired the swans' **8)** _____

and then took her sister home.

Use the Word List above to choose the correct word for each meaning. Write your choice on the line.

9. beauty and grace _____

10. without letting up _____

11. thrilled _____

12. young swans _____

13. considered _____

14. thinking of only one thing _____

15. believe; understand _____

16. great mental distress _____

Recipe Rewards

Lindsay thought that it was sad that they were selling all of Mrs. Stanton's things, but she went to the auction because she wanted to buy something of Mrs. Stanton's that could help her remember her neighbor.

When the little tin box was auctioned off, only Lindsay knew what was in it; and she got it for a quarter. "It holds all of Mrs. Stanton's recipes," she told Lester. "You know what a wonderful cook she was. This is a gold mine!"

"I've figured out how to print our neighborhood newspaper," Lester said, acting as though he hadn't even heard her. "We can use Mother's word processor, and Dad says we can print it on his laser printer for about two cents a sheet!"

By Friday, the first issue of *The Blab* was almost written. "We'll distribute this one free," Lester said. Lindsay wanted to know how they would do that. "I'm not a delivery person!" she said.

Lester had an idea. "The town newspapers are dropped on the corner for John Beld to deliver," he said. "Before he gets there, we'll slip *The Blab* into each copy. Then we'll get busy on the next issue."

"Who's going to dig up new news?" Lindsay groaned.

Lester had another idea. Quickly he squeezed one more item into *The Blab*. "Call 555-3250 with a news story," it said, "and get a free recipe over the phone."

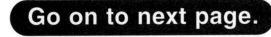

Go on to next page.

Directions

Answer each question about the passage. Circle the letter in front of the correct answer.

1. Lindsay gets Mrs. Stanton's recipes _____.
   a. out of a newspaper
   b. over the phone
   c. at an auction
   d. from Lester's mother

2. Mrs. Stanton's recipes are "a gold mine" because she _____.
   a. wrote for the town newspaper
   b. kept them in a gold box
   c. was known as a good cook
   d. auctioned them off

3. *The Blab* is printed at _____.
   a. the town newspaper office
   b. Lester's house
   c. Mrs. Stanton's house
   d. John Beld's house

4. Lester could be called a boy who _____.
   a. has many ideas
   b. is a good cook
   c. never listens
   d. delivers newspapers

5. Lindsay is not interested in putting out *The Blab* if _____.
   a. Lester is writing it
   b. John Beld is going to deliver it
   c. it is printed on a laser printer
   d. doing it is too much work

Vegetable Void

When Corey's family moved to an apartment in the city, he knew there would be many changes. The peaceful countryside that he was used to had been replaced by busy city thoroughfares and tall buildings. Gone were the wide-open vistas and the sounds of nature that he used to see and hear. In the city, the traffic and the people moved in constant streams past his high-rise, and the steady noise flowed into his window day and night.

Soon, Corey realized that he would miss something else. His family had always had large gardens in which they grew all sorts of vegetables. He loved their fresh taste, especially the tomatoes. The ones that his mother brought home from the markets in the city just didn't taste the same. When he mentioned it, his mother said he would have to get used to it, because as he could see, there was no room for a garden in the city.

It seemed the more he thought about it, the more he could taste those tomatoes. He thought there must be some way that he could grow some tomatoes. He found some large buckets and bought some potting soil. Then he bought some tomato seedlings and planted them in the buckets. He put the buckets out on the balcony where they would get plenty of sunlight during the day. His mother smiled to herself when she saw the buckets. She missed the taste of homegrown vegetables, too. She hoped his plants would flourish.

Corey tended his plants daily. He removed the suckers that grew between the branches and made sure the plants were kept watered and had support so that they would not fall over. Soon the plants had small yellow blossoms. By the end of the summer, there were healthy green tomatoes growing on the plants; and soon afterward, the sun turned the tomatoes bright red. When Corey harvested his first tomatoes, he and his mother ate them like apples, savoring their flavor while the juice ran down their chins. It seemed that nothing else had ever tasted so sweet!

Go on to next page.

Directions

Answer each question about the story. Circle the letter in front of the correct answer.

1. What did Corey miss most about living in the city?
   a. the quiet of the country
   b. weeding his garden
   c. the taste of fresh tomatoes
   d. the wide-open vistas

2. How did Corey's mother feel about his tomato plants?
   a. She thought he was being foolish.
   b. She knew they would not grow.
   c. She did not care for tomatoes.
   d. She was looking forward to the tomatoes.

3. Where did Corey grow the tomatoes?
   a. on the balcony
   b. in his room
   c. in the kitchen
   d. in the garden

4. How did Corey and his mother eat the first tomatoes?
   a. They put them in a salad.
   b. They cut them up and ate them.
   c. They made them into juice.
   d. They bit right into them.

Write _true_ or _false_ next to each sentence.

5. _____ Corey's new home was very different from his old one.

6. _____ Corey's mother did not buy vegetables in the city.

7. _____ The tomato plants needed sun, water, and support.

8. _____ Corey grew the plants in window boxes.

9. _____ His attempts to grow tomatoes did not succeed.

10. _____ Corey and his mother ate the ripe tomatoes like apples.

Taping Time

One day in October, Roger had to stay home from school because he did not feel well. During the day, he noticed the sun through his window making a shadow that moved across the room as the hours passed.

The next morning, Roger awakened before the sun came up. He was feeling better, but his mother said he should stay home one more day. When the sun came up, Roger marked the shadow on the floor with white tape. "When it's at this spot each day," he said, "I need to get up and get ready for school."

During the day, Roger watched the clock by his bed and put a piece of tape at the shadow on the floor every hour. Then he would write something on the tape like "Be ready to leave for school," "Getting out our spelling books at school," or "Have hands washed for supper."

The next morning, Roger used his tape clock to get up and off to school. The morning after that was cloudy, and he had to rely on his regular clock, but the tape clock worked quite well for a couple of weeks.

Then one morning, Roger came down to breakfast a bit late. "You're running late today," his father said. "You'll have to hurry to make it to school on time." Suddenly Roger remembered that the position of the sun when seen from Earth changes every day, so the shadow is in a different place. His tape clock was no longer accurate.

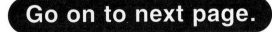

Go on to next page.

Directions

Answer each question about the story. Circle the letter in front of the correct answer.

1. Roger gets the idea for his tape clock one day when he is _____.
   a. reading about old sundials
   b. sitting in school
   c. staying home from school
   d. having his breakfast

2. Roger compares the numbers on his regular clock to the _____.
   a. sun in the sky
   b. movement of people on the street
   c. shadows on the floor
   d. words on the tape

3. On a piece of tape, Roger writes _____.
   a. what he is usually doing at that time
   b. the hour it stands for
   c. a note to his mother
   d. what his mother is doing

4. Roger's clock doesn't work on cloudy days because _____.
   a. he stays home from school those days
   b. the tape doesn't stick to the floor
   c. he has to keep his window closed
   d. the sun can't make the shadow

5. Soon the tape clock is unreliable because _____.
   a. the times he does things change
   b. the sun's position changes
   c. someone moves the piece of tape
   d. the shadow disappears forever

Party Surprise

Penny had promised her mother that she would help with her little brother's birthday party Saturday afternoon. She was looking forward to it because her mother always had interesting things going on at the parties she gave. There was never a dull moment. That, said her mother, was the secret to keeping a roomful of young children in some kind of order and having a good birthday party.

On Saturday morning, Penny got up and began to help her mother put together the prize bags and other surprises that she had made or bought earlier in the week. Seven children had been invited, but only five parents had responded. Still, they planned for all seven children, plus Jack, Penny's brother. They put whistles, gliders, peanuts, taffy, and other small items in the prize bags. There were three larger prizes for game winners. Penny and her mother blew up balloons and strung streamers. By the time the children arrived for the party, Penny and her mother were ready for anything, or so they thought!

As the children began to play their first game, Penny noticed something odd. It seemed that an extra child had materialized at the party! She decided she must have counted incorrectly, so she counted again—still nine! When she got a chance, she mentioned it to her mother, who also counted heads. "We'll have to figure out this mystery later, Penny," said her mother. "For now, please go fix the goody bags so that there are enough for nine children!"

Penny went into the kitchen and looked at the tray that held the bags. How could she make another bag so that all the bags would be even? She opened the bags and counted. There were nine items in each bag, and she had to make another bag. She got out some paper and did some figuring. A multiplication problem told her that eight bags with nine items each were the equivalent of seventy-two items. She tried a division problem to find the number that would make each bag equal. Her calculation worked! Happily, Penny filled the nine bags, and went back to the party, giving her mother the all-clear signal.

Later, they found out that Jack had invited another friend without telling anyone. "Kids!" thought Penny. "Don't they know how much planning goes into these parties?"

Go on to next page.

Directions

Read each clue. Choose a word from the story that best fits each clue. Write the words in the puzzle.

ACROSS
4. the mathematical process of dividing
5. the mathematical process of multiplying
6. a sign that everything is all right
8. wrongly

DOWN
1. appeared suddenly
2. equal to
3. figuring; something figured by calculating
7. as many as will fill a room

Just Plane Crazy

Maxie had read all about people who had tried to make airplanes. He also read about hang gliders that looked like big kites and floated around mountains.

"You're too young to fly," his father said. "We'll see about getting flying lessons when you're older."

"I know I can do it," Maxie thought. "I will just have to make my own glider plane." He looked around and found some things he thought he could use.

Maxie took the wheels off his old soapbox racer. He also cut the heavy canvas off the frame. Then he made a huge kite with an old bedsheet and fishing poles and tied it to the racer with clothesline.

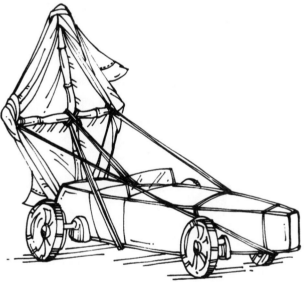

When he was ready, Maxie had to put the wheels back on long enough to pull the contraption way up to the top of Markers Point. Ted Squires saw him going up and ran lickety-split to tell Maxie's father.

When his father got up to Markers Point, Maxie had the wheels off again and was trying to figure out how to shove the thing off the cliff and jump in at the same time. "Are you crazy?" his father screamed.

"Aw!" Maxie said. "This thing will fly itself."

"Fine," his father said. He picked up Maxie's airplane and tossed it over the cliff. It fell like a bag of potatoes straight down into the gully. "Too bad, Maxie," his father said. "I forgot to give you time to get in. Let's go down and have a look at it."

Go on to next page.

Directions

Answer each question about the story. Circle the letter in front of the correct answer.

1. Maxie makes his glider plane by _____.
   a. following the plans for hang gliders
   b. using exactly what other inventors used
   c. using things he found lying around
   d. studying modern airplanes

2. The body of Maxie's plane is made from _____.
   a. some fishing poles
   b. heavy canvas
   c. a potato bag
   d. a soapbox racer

3. If it weren't for Ted Squires, Maxie would have been _____.
   a. flying his plane around Markers Point
   b. down in the gully with his plane
   c. home reading about airplanes
   d. rebuilding his soapbox racer

4. Maxie puts the wheels back on his plane to _____.
   a. get it up to Markers Point
   b. roll it home after it fell
   c. race it in the derby
   d. roll it off the cliff

5. Maxie's father is trying to show Maxie _____.
   a. how to make a plane that would fly
   b. that Ted Squires should mind his own business
   c. that making the plane is a big mistake
   d. how hang gliders work

An Eye for Detail

Fanny told her friends that their school team would win the game for sure.

"How can you know that?" Ben asked. "We're four points behind, and the game is almost over." But sure enough, Wilson Tuller, the other team's star player, had to leave the game with a sore ankle. Without his playing, Fanny and Ben's school won the game by two points.

Fanny thought it strange that her friends hadn't noticed that Wilson Tuller had started limping before she predicted they would win. She always noticed things like that.

Before they got out of the gym, Fanny suggested that they call one of their parents and get a ride home. "Why?" Betty demanded.

"I'm fairly sure it's pouring rain outside," Fanny said. No one believed her. But sure enough, when they got to the door, it was pouring cats and dogs.

"You must have bad knees or something," Sam said laughing.

Betty looked behind them and could still see the lady who had just come into the gym and passed them carrying a folded, dripping umbrella.

"You ought to be a fortune teller!" Ben said.

"Actually," Fanny said, "I'm thinking of becoming a detective."

"If you say so, then it's sure to happen," Ben said.

Go on to next page.

Directions

Answer each question about the story. Circle the letter in front of the correct answer.

1. Fanny could predict that her team would win the game because she _____.
   a. is a fortune teller
   b. knows a lot about the game
   c. had noticed Wilson Tuller limping
   d. makes a guess and is lucky

2. Fanny knows that it is raining because _____.
   a. rain always makes her knees hurt
   b. she has seen someone come in with a wet umbrella
   c. she had sneaked out and then come back in
   d. she had felt a drip from a leaky roof

3. No one believes Fanny when she says it is raining because they _____.
   a. are tired of her always being right
   b. had just come in from outside
   c. think she is guessing
   d. could not see outside from inside the gym

4. Ben thinks that Fanny should be a fortune teller because he believes that she _____.
   a. notices a lot of details
   b. has the power to predict the future
   c. always gets her way
   d. has a crystal ball hidden somewhere

5. Fanny thinks she would make a good detective because detectives _____.
   a. need to pay attention to details
   b. are always predicting the future
   c. know when to stay out of the rain
   d. can predict how games will end

Burglar Bungle

Jerry never forgot the day they had all the excitement at their house. It was a Sunday afternoon. Jerry's dad, a police officer, was at work driving his squad car. Jerry's mom had taken his little sisters and his grandmother to the afternoon movies. Jerry was more interested in being out with his friends than going to the movies.

In the middle of the afternoon, Jerry returned home to get some money. While he was looking for his extra cash, he heard noises upstairs. Jerry thought the noises sounded like drawers opening and closing. "That's funny," he mused. "I thought everyone was out." So he went to the bottom of the stairs and called, "Who's up there?" There was no response. He called again. Nothing.

At this point Jerry decided that he had a problem. If burglars were upstairs, he was not inclined to go up and confront them. So he ran outside, leaving the front door open, and rushed next door to the Danners' house. On hearing his problem, Mr. Danner called the police. Then, armed with a baseball bat, he accompanied Jerry back to the house.

Meanwhile, the call about the burglar was radioed to Jerry's dad's squad car. "What's going on?" he cried to his partner. "That's my house! Move it!"

By the time the squad car reached the house, Mr. Danner was just coming downstairs, dragging his bat and looking annoyed. Jerry followed, a sheepish grin on his face. "It's all right!" he called, seeing his dad rush up the walk.

"It was just Grandma," Jerry explained when everyone had gathered in the entryway. "She didn't go with Mom and the girls to the movies. Instead, she came over here to pack up some things for Mom to take to Goodwill. She had her hearing aid turned down and didn't hear a thing when I called upstairs!"

So everything had turned out all right after all. Jerry's dad was relieved, and Jerry had a good story to tell his mom when she returned. The only disgruntled member of the "rescue team" was Mr. Danner, who had sincerely wanted to catch a burglar and be on the six o'clock news.

Go on to next page.

Name_____   Date_____

Directions

Think about the passage you read. Then fill in the blanks of the following paragraph with words from the Word List.

Word List
squad   burglars   sheepish   bungle
inclined   entryway   disgruntled   confront

When Jerry heard noises upstairs, he thought there were **1)** _____ in his house.

He was not **2)** _____ to go upstairs. He did not want to **3)** _____

the burglars alone. He ran to his neighbor's house, and his neighbor called the police. Jerry's father

heard the call on the radio of his **4)** _____ car. When Jerry's dad got to the house,

Jerry and Mr. Danner were coming down the stairs. Jerry looked **5)** _____, and

Mr. Danner was **6)** _____. As they stood in the **7)** _____, Jerry

explained that it was not burglars, but his grandmother who was upstairs. It had been a burglar

8) _____!

Write *fact* or *opinion* in front of each sentence about the passage.

9. _____ Jerry's father is a police officer.

10. _____ It is not fun to go to the afternoon movies.

11. _____ It is foolish to confront burglars in your house.

12. _____ Mr. Danner is Jerry's neighbor.

13. _____ Mr. Danner brought a bat with him for protection.

14. _____ Jerry should have made sure it was a burglar before alarming everyone.

15. _____ Mr. Danner was upset because he wanted to be on the news.

Celia's Scare

Celia had a very odd feeling. She didn't feel alone in her room. It was as though someone was watching her, but she was the only person there. She knew that no one could be looking in her window because her room was on the second floor, high off the ground.

As soon as Celia went downstairs, the feeling went away. It was Saturday, and she had breakfast and then watched some television. Then she went outside. Maximilian, the big gray cat that lived several houses away, came ambling up. "Hi, Max," she said, scratching the cat's head. Maximilian yawned and ambled away as though he were bored.

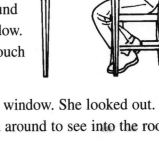

"I guess I'll read the book about Clara Barton," Celia thought, heading up to her room. She settled into a big chair with the book. Soon Celia had the uneasy feeling again. "There must be someone in here," she thought. "I can feel someone watching me!"

She sat forward in the chair, holding her breath, and looked all around the room. Just then she thought she saw something move past the window. She got up slowly and began shaking a little as she moved in a half-crouch toward the window.

Celia's heart almost stopped when a fluffy gray tail wafted past the window. She looked out. There at the end of the window ledge sat Maximilian, craning his head around to see into the room. "You rascal!" Celia cried. "You really gave me a scare!"

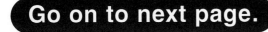

Go on to next page.

Directions

Answer each question about the story. Circle the letter in front of the correct answer.

1. Celia has an odd feeling when she is _____.
   a. scratching Maximilian's head
   b. having her breakfast
   c. watching television
   d. alone in her room

2. When Celia feels odd, she thinks she is _____.
   a. acting silly
   b. being watched
   c. on television
   d. reading too much

3. As Celia begins moving toward the window, she feels _____.
   a. afraid
   b. happy
   c. relieved
   d. sad

4. Celia is being watched by _____.
   a. Clara
   b. her mother
   c. Maximilian
   d. a friend

5. At the end of the story, Celia decides that Maximilian isn't _____.
   a. a very good climber
   b. very interested in knowing what she is doing
   c. the cat she saw sitting on the window
   d. as bored with her as he acts outside

Lost Louis

Shortly after I moved to Florida, I bought a condominium. It had an eat-in kitchen, two large bedrooms, two full baths, a "great room'" with vaulted ceilings and skylights, and a wonderful screened porch overlooking the tennis courts. I mention the layout only because it was perfect for my cats Fleur de Lis and Louis IX to run and play in. They were used to my one-bedroom condo up North; and although they loved summer walks on the beach, they always had to spend the winter indoors. Now, however, they had infinitely more room to play in PLUS the screened porch to use all year round. They were thrilled.

The day we moved in I was busy unpacking and cleaning, so Fleur and Louis decided to play "box." In cat play talk, this means vaulting into every available carton, flinging out the top layer, and burrowing snugly somewhere between the second layer and the bottom. If a box happened to hold soft socks or towels, so much the better.

I finished unpacking just as it began to rain. Closing the last drawer, I suddenly wondered where the cats were. Fleur was behind me on the bed, but Louis was nowhere in sight. Knowing how he loved to hide, I checked all his usual places. No luck. I tried the kitchen cabinets, under the sink, and behind the sofa. Zero.

Now I was worried. Maybe he got out the door. Maybe he ran into the street. MAYBE HE IS IN A CARTON IN THE DUMPSTER!

Totally panic-stricken, I ran out into the street in the pouring rain and nearly got run over by a van. No Louis. Then I fled to the dumpster and clambered to the top. Scarred from my ascent but feeling no pain, I scrabbled at the cartons, shouting Louis's name and listening for meows. Nothing.

Finally, soaking wet, smelling of garbage, and sobbing out loud, I went back home. Hardly knowing what I did, I peeled off my jacket and reached into the closet for a robe. And then I heard it. From under some Northern woolies piled and ready for storage, came a loud, contented purr.

Go on to next page.

Name_____ Date_____

Directions

Read each sentence. Choose a word from the Word List that has the same meaning as the word or words in bold print. Write the word on the line.

Word List

vaulting   panic-stricken   ascent   scrabbled
layout   clambered   infinitely   storage

1. The author's new home had a very different **floor plan** than his old one. _____

2. The new place had **limitlessly** more space than his old home. _____

3. His cats enjoyed **leaping** into the empty cartons as he unpacked._____

4. Suddenly, he was **terribly frightened** at the thought that he may have thrown Louis out with the trash. _____

5. He **climbed** to the top of the dumpster. _____

6. The **climb up to the top** scratched him, but he did not feel it. _____

7. After he **pawed around** through the boxes, he sadly went home. _____

8. As he got a robe from **extra space for putting things away,** he heard Louis._____

Write true or false next to each sentence.

9. _____ The author had just moved to Florida.

10. _____ The new home was much larger than the old one.

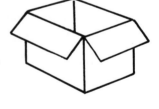

11. _____ The author's cat, Fleur, was missing.

12. _____ The author had thrown him in the dumpster.

13. _____ The cats were both hiding in the storage area.

14. _____ The author was hurt while climbing into the dumpster.

15. _____ Louis was in the storage area, unharmed.

Alfonso's New Home

Felix rubbed Alfonso's head gently after placing him in the low basket that MaryAnn had prepared for the puppy. "I can't stay," Felix said. "We're leaving for vacation first thing in the morning, and I think I'm catching a cold. Dad says I have to get right to bed," Felix said, sniffling. MaryAnn noticed that his eyes were red and were starting to water.

"He didn't have to give me the dog," MaryAnn said after Felix turned abruptly—almost without saying good-bye—and left. "He knows I'd look after Alfonso for him while his family is away." She was very suspicious. "Felix always wants something whenever he gives you anything," she thought.

MaryAnn's mother said, "Maybe someone is allergic over at Felix's house, or maybe Felix doesn't like the dog as much as he lets on."

MaryAnn's father suggested that taking care of a puppy had turned out to be more trouble than Felix had anticipated. "Little League will be started when he gets back, and that takes a lot of time."

As soon as Felix returned from vacation, he came by. He sat quietly patting Alfonso until MaryAnn blurted out, "Felix, I have to know! Why did you give Alfonso to me?"

"Why do you think?" Felix asked.

MaryAnn told him all of the possible reasons she had thought of.

"I love Alfonso!" Felix said firmly. "But the veterinarian says that Alfonso is allergic to our new carpet. It gives him a rash. So I needed someone to give Alfonso a good home, and you've certainly done that."

Go on to next page.

Directions

Answer each question about the story. Circle the letter in front of the correct answer.

1. MaryAnn thinks that Felix gave her the dog because he _____.
   a. wants something in return
   b. is allergic to Alfonso
   c. doesn't have time to take care of the dog
   d. doesn't really like the dog

2. Felix leaves MaryAnn's house abruptly because _____.
   a. the dog is giving him a rash
   b. he is afraid that MaryAnn will not keep Alfonso
   c. he is afraid that he is going to cry
   d. he has to go to Little League practice

3. The reader can tell that Felix loves Alfonso because he _____.
   a. prepares a bed for the dog
   b. pets the dog gently and comes to visit him
   c. leaves for vacation
   d. goes home to bed

4. A good word to describe the way MaryAnn feels when Felix gives her the dog is _____.
   a. unhappy
   b. victorious
   c. angry
   d. suspicious

5. The reason that Felix gives MaryAnn the dog is that _____.
   a. he wants to borrow something from her
   b. he has to leave for vacation
   c. Alfonso is allergic to the family's new carpet
   d. Little League practice takes too much of his time

Troy's Home!

Troy was so excessively neat that his family and friends sometimes kidded him about it. He just liked things to be in order and arranged in such a manner that he could find whatever he needed without the inconvenience of digging through piles. Some of his friend's rooms looked as though some catastrophe had taken place in them, the way the clothes, sports equipment, and books were thrown all over the place. If he mentioned it, they would say, "What do you mean?" Not only could Troy find things quickly, he always knew if someone else had been in his room. He never got upset about it if he found things misplaced; he simply returned them to their proper place.

Consequently, for some time now, Troy had been noticing his resource materials out of place. He usually had them lined up from tallest to shortest, but often when he returned from school, he would find them rearranged or disheveled in some other way. He would put them back in order, hardly thinking about it, and then the next day they'd be moved again! He began to wonder what was going on. His mother wouldn't be cleaning house that often, and she didn't need to be looking at his books—she had plenty of her own. His brother, Jason, was much too young to be interested in his books yet, and he wasn't supposed to be in Troy's room anyway.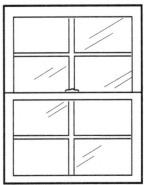

Then one day when Troy came home, he found the books out of the shelf and piled up near his window. He walked over and stood considering the pile for a moment, and suddenly he thought he knew what had been happening. He called to Jason, who came running enthusiastically but stopped short, looking at the pile of books. His eyes got very large, and he put his hand over his mouth. "Oops!" he said.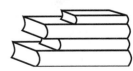

"Show me what you do," said Troy.

Jason stepped up onto the pile of books and stretched his neck to the window. "Then the bus comes, and Troy's home!" he exclaimed, smiling from ear to ear. Troy picked him up and gave him a hug. "We'll have to find you a stool," he said, smiling. "That's too much work!"

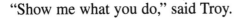

Go on to next page.

Name_____ Date_____

Directions

Read each clue. Choose a word from the story to fit each clue. Write the words in the puzzle.

ACROSS

1. causing bother or trouble
6. with great eagerness
7. changed the position of
8. to a great extent; too much so

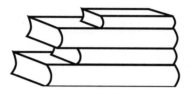

DOWN

2. therefore
3. a great and sudden calamity
4. something of use
5. untidy

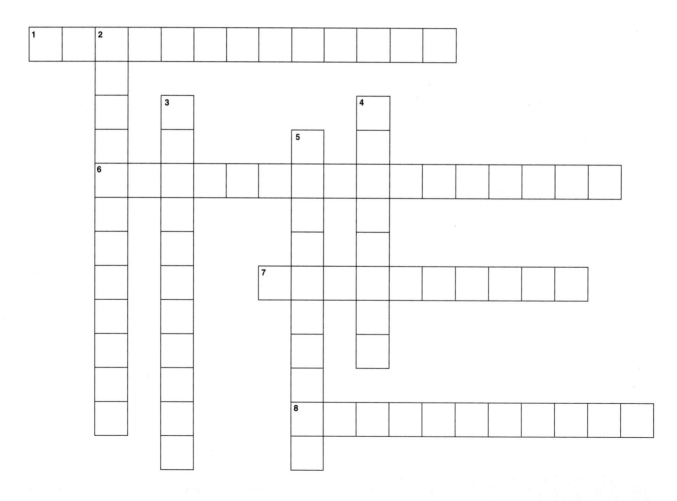

Dragging Her Feet

On Friday, as usual, Matthew and his little sister, Jennifer, were walking to school. As usual, Jennifer was excited about starting her day. Dragging his feet, Matthew grumbled, "Why is she always so eager to get there? School is school. It won't disappear or anything if we take our time."

Usually Jennifer ran ahead of him, sometimes skipping or hopping for a short way, sometimes stopping to pick up a brightly colored leaf or smell a flower. Now, however, she lagged behind, and he had to turn around to make sure she was there. "She's kind of slow today," Matthew remarked to no one in particular. "She's even slower than I am."

A block later Jennifer was still lagging behind, and Matthew had to stop to let her catch up with him. "What's the matter, Jenny?" he teased. "Got a big test today?"

"No tests in kindergarten!" exclaimed Jennifer, making a funny face. She tried to hop, but couldn't seem to manage it.

"Well, let's get a move on, then!" he urged. "I don't want to be late. Mr. Keller has a Little League sign-up sheet that's just begging for my name!"

At the school crossing, Matthew had to turn again and wait for Jennifer. He noticed her strange gait but dismissed it as play. "C'mon on, Jenny!" he called. "The guard can't keep the cars waiting all day!"

At last they reached the schoolyard. Although Jennifer usually ran ahead of him to the kindergarten play area, today Matthew practically had to haul her there.

Suddenly Jennifer cried, "Hey, there's Miss Estapa!" and hobbled off. Curious, Matthew followed. Jennifer was babbling in a high, excited voice, so it was only after hearing her last breathless phrase that he looked down at her feet. "—AND I GOT DRESSED ALL BY MYSELF TODAY!" explained everything.

Go on to next page.

Directions

Answer each question about the story. Circle the letter in front of the correct answer.

1. Jennifer usually hops and skips to school because she _____.
   a. wants to take as long as possible to get there
   b. likes Fridays
   c. enjoys kindergarten
   d. has a wild imagination

2. When Matthew says that his teacher has a sign-up sheet just begging for his name, he means that _____.
   a. he is eager to sign up for Little League
   b. the sign-up sheet is on videotape
   c. a computer has selected him to be on the team
   d. Mr. Keller has asked him to join

3. The word *gait* in the story probably means _____.
   a. an opening in a fence
   b. a way of walking
   c. something that Jennifer is wearing
   d. a funny face

4. Matthew follows Jennifer to her teacher's side because he _____.
   a. is afraid Jennifer might fall
   b. wants to talk to Miss Estapa
   c. no longer cares about the Little League sign-up sheet
   d. wants to hear what Jennifer will tell her

5. Jennifer's words "explain everything" by telling Matthew that she _____.
   a. feels grown-up because she dressed herself
   b. really does have a test today
   c. has her shoes on the wrong feet
   d. is ready for first grade

Improving Reading Comprehension
Grade 6

Answer Key

Pp. 7-8
1. preoccupied
2. ministers
3. admirable
4. momentary
5. crisis
6. b
7. c
8. b
9. unexpectedly
10. preoccupied
11. admirable
Answers will vary.
Students should use
complete sentences
and support their
statements.

Pp. 9-10
1. assaulted
2. mid-flight
3. ascertain
4. explanation
5. disturbances
6. assaulted
7. high-pitched
8. accompanied
9. mid-flight
10. ascertain
11. false
12. true
13. true
14. false
15. false
Answers will vary.
Students should use
complete sentences
and address
questions.

P. 12
1. b
2. a
3. d
4. b
5. c

P. 14
1. preoccupied
2. prime ministers
3. admirable (or
momentary)
4. crisis
5. momentary (or
admirable)
6. attentive
7. guidance
8. anxiety
9. attentive
10. momentary
11. preoccupied
12. crisis
13. guidance
14. admirable
15. anxiety
16. prime ministers

P. 16
1. d
2. c
3. b
4. a
5. a

P. 18
1. b
2. a
3. c
4. d
5. true
6. false
7. true
8. false
9. true
10. false

P. 20
1. b
2. a
3. d
4. a
5. b

P. 22
ACROSS
3. curriculum
5. isolated
6. majority
7. employed
DOWN
1. increasingly
2. specialized
3. concepts
4. violence

P. 24
1. b
2. d
3. c
4. a
5. b

P. 26
1. c
2. d
3. a
4. a
5. b

P. 28
1. catwalk
2. cowcatcher
3. fateful
4. caboose
5. right-of-way
6. throttle
7. sandbox
8. locomotive
Answers will vary.

P. 30
1. d
2. c
3. a
4. d
5. c

P. 32
1. feverish
2. conscience
3. scorched
4. rightful
5. false
6. true
7. true
8. true
9. true
10. false
Answers will vary.

P. 34
1. b
2. a
3. c
4. d
5. a

P. 36
ACROSS
3. legendary
4. storytelling
7. minstrels
8. sagas
DOWN
1. literature
2. conveys
5. enrich
6. climax

P. 38
1. b
2. d
3. b
4. b
5. c

P. 40
1. c
2. a
3. b
4. c
5. d

P. 42
ACROSS
2. disposal
4. appreciative
7. acquainted
8. resources
DOWN
1. cataloguing
3. ingenuity
5. prominent
6. vehicle

P. 44
1. a
2. c
3. b
4. b
5. d

P. 46
1. rambling
2. encountered
3. destination
4. overhanging
5. backroads
6. backpacking
7. revisit
8. collective

P. 48
1. d
2. c
3. b
4. c
5. a

P. 50
1. ridiculing
2. bewilderment
3. interpretation
4. diversity
5. individuality
6. breakthroughs
7. peer
8. niche
9. opinion
10. fact
11. opinion
12. fact
13. opinion
14. fact
15. opinion

P. 52
1. b
2. b
3. d
4. c
5. c

P. 54
1. d
2. a
3. b
4. c
5. a

P. 56
1. irritably
2. exasperated
3. asunder
4. discount
5. crestfallen
6. recollection
7. imaginable
8. enthusiastically
9. true
10. false
11. false
12. false
13. true
14. true
15. true
16. false

P. 58
1. b
2. a
3. d
4. The poem gets smaller and smaller as the author asks the question about all things disappearing.
5. Poems will vary.

P. 60
ACROSS
2. embers
4. appreciative
7. early-morning
8. ominous
DOWN
1. disagreeable
3. boisterous
5. embankment
6. hardwoods

P. 62
1. a
2. c
3. d
4. c
5. d

P. 64
1. intrusion
2. cherished
3. craziness
4. inclination
5. ecstatic
6. true
7. false
8. true
9. true
10. true
11. true

P. 66
1. d
2. b
3. d
4. a
5. a

P. 68
1. d
2. a
3. c
4. b
5. c

P. 70
1. distraction
2. pondered
3. persistently
4. preoccupation
5. conceive
6. elated
7. cygnets
8. elegance
9. elegance
10. persistently
11. elated
12. cygnets
13. pondered
14. preoccupation
15. conceive
16. distraction

P. 72
1. c
2. c
3. b
4. a
5. d

P. 74
1. c
2. d
3. a
4. d
5. true
6. false
7. true
8. false
9. false
10. true

P. 76
1. c
2. c
3. a
4. d
5. b

P. 78
ACROSS
4. division
5. multiplication
6. all-clear
8. incorrectly
DOWN
1. materialized
2. equivalent
3. calculation
7. roomful

P. 80
1. c
2. d
3. b
4. a
5. c

P. 82
1. c
2. b
3. d
4. b
5. a

P. 84
1. burglars
2. inclined
3. confront
4. squad
5. sheepish
6. disgruntled
7. entryway
8. bungle
9. fact
10. opinion
11. opinion
12. fact
13. fact
14. opinion
15. fact

P. 86
1. d
2. b
3. a
4. c
5. d

P. 88
1. layout
2. infinitely
3. vaulting
4. panic-stricken
5. clambered
6. ascent
7. scrabbled
8. storage
9. true
10. true
11. false
12. false
13. false
14. true
15. true

P. 90
1. a
2. c
3. b
4. d
5. c

P. 92
ACROSS
1. inconvenience
6. enthusiastically
7. rearranged
8. excessively
DOWN
2. consequently
3. catastrophe
4. resource
5. disheveled

P. 94
1. c
2. a
3. b
4. d
5. c